The Opium Queen

THE OPIUM QUEEN

*The Untold Story of the Rebel Who
Ruled the Golden Triangle*

GABRIELLE PALUCH

ROWMAN & LITTLEFIELD
Lanham • Boulder • New York • London

Published by Rowman & Littlefield
An imprint of The Rowman & Littlefield Publishing Group, Inc.
4501 Forbes Boulevard, Suite 200, Lanham, Maryland 20706
www.rowman.com

86-90 Paul Street, London EC2A 4NE, United Kingdom

British Library Cataloguing in Publication Information available

Library of Congress Cataloging-in-Publication Data
Names: Paluch, Gabrielle, 1985- author.
Title: The opium queen : the untold story of the rebel who ruled the Golden
    Triangle / Gabrielle Paluch.
Description: Lanham : Rowman & Littlefield, [2023] | Includes index. |
    Summary: "Opium Queen is the true story of the widely mythologized
    genderqueer Burmese opium-pioneer of noble Chinese descent, Olive Yang,
    who secretly ran an anti-communist rebel army supported by the CIA in
    the 1950s heyday of the Golden Triangle"—Provided by publisher.
Identifiers: LCCN 2022041067 (print) | LCCN 2022041068 (ebook) |
    ISBN 9781538131978 (cloth) | ISBN 9781538131985 (epub)
Subjects: LCSH: Yang, Olive, 1927-2017. | Opium trade—Golden Triangle
    (Southeast Asia)—History—20th century. | Gender-nonconforming
    people—Burma—Biography.
Classification: LCC DS526.9 .P35 2023 (print) | LCC DS526.9 (ebook) |
    DDC 959.05/1092 [B]—dc23/eng/20220914
LC record available at https://lccn.loc.gov/2022041067
LC ebook record available at https://lccn.loc.gov/2022041068

On Kokang

Beneath those lofty Kokang peaks,
There is hardly any pleasure to seek.
Faint mule tracks are the only ways
To Kokang's heart by monotonous days.

By monsoon season ways turn to pools,
And skillful riders become fools,
Slipping down with thunderous sound.
When riders and horses fall asunder,
Legs and hands become broken members.

By day the Kunlong Valley bears great heat,
By night mosquitoes wander in great fleets.
But noisy and bright are market days,
When Shan belles don on colours light and gay.

The clumsy movement of stubborn mules
Adds much curiosity to one's view.
And petty merchants fat, big, and small,
All yelling beside wooden stalls.

Scaling down from the high hill crags,
Are the inhabitants in jet-blue black,
All carrying baskets and big brown sacks.
While swooping down, they look like clowns,
With animals making lugubrious sounds.

—*Puck Hee Lee*, chief medical officer
of Kokang, 1952–1963

Contents

Contents

Preface

W HEN O LIVE Y ANG DIED IN 2017, THE WORLD LOST THE REMARKABLE untold true story of a complex antihero who was so widely mythologized as to be misunderstood. It also lost a repository of secrets and stories about how covert Central Intelligence Agency operations in Burma in the 1950s gave rise to the modern narcotics trade of the Golden Triangle, impacted the Sino-Burmese border agreement, and ushered in the Burmese military era.

This is the story of Olive, the Yang family, and a place called Kokang. This is also the story of how secrets about Olive Yang took on a life of their own against the backdrop of an important theater of the United States' Cold War against China. This is also a story of propaganda and lies, and what truths they reflect back to us.

Olive became a living legend by the age of thirty, as the Golden Triangle became the center of the global narcotics trade. Olive was running an incredibly successful trading caravan in Burma's Shan State, with a racket rumored to be the driving force behind the unprecedented amount of opium being produced. Olive's business became so lucrative, large loads of gold bars began to pile up in trunks around her house.

Olive had been named as an arms-smuggler for CIA-supported anti-communist guerillas in a complaint filed at the United Nations General Assembly in 1953. As those guerillas continued their clandestine attacks against communist China along the disputed border, they continued to support themselves through their opium sales. Olive's men were said to have burned villages and murdered government officials. Olive was said to rule the security staff for the opium caravans and extractive businesses like a dictator, putting delinquent employees in cages, and sometimes forcing them into a life of crime on penalty of death.

The allure of Olive's feminine power inspired a British crime novelist in 1957. He wrote about his lurid adventure to find the abominable criminal mastermind and seductress, who tortured her soldiers with burning needles to satisfy sexually sadistic desires in her constant opium-laced stupor.

Then, in 1961, another novel was published, this time in Chinese, about the plight of the guerillas in their resistance against the communists on the Burmese border with China, in which Olive appeared as a Chinese Joan of Arc and selfless martyr.

By the time the Yang family was purged, Olive had played a significant role in raising the generation of opium warlords who made the Golden Triangle infamous, and supplied the majority of the world's heroin for over a decade.

While events in novels and memoirs were fictionalized and names were changed, enough details remained true to life that sophisticated readers were still able to recognize Olive in their pages. Olive remained a subject of public fascination and geopolitical importance. But no first-person accounts seemed to emerge, and so fact and fiction were easily confused. Some wanted to believe Olive was a hero, some wanted to believe Olive was a villain. To the family who shared weddings, funerals, and gossip with Olive, some of the stories were baffling—some because they were true, some because they weren't.

The most interesting things about Olive were never really secret. The fascinating details of Olive's life are scattered in novels and archives, waiting to be discovered. Many questions about Olive are left unanswered in this book, because most of Kokang's archival record has been either destroyed or classified.

The Myanmar National Archives house the majority of the classified government records of Kokang from Olive's time in power—though many were destroyed. These were made partially available to me but not as broadly as to now-deceased Shan scholar Sai Kham Mong, a longtime lecturer at Mandalay University. Particularly, records pertaining to Olive's arrest in Myanmar in 1962 remain secret. Chinese Communist Party records, other than the ones gazetted by government historians like Lu Chengwang in Kunming, are not available to the public.

Though Olive was never a salaried employee of the so-called Secret Army, records at the National Archives of Taiwan contain a wealth of detail about many of Olive's trade routes. Many of those records were only recently declassified.

The untold stories contained in these records may have benefited people at the CIA, who later modeled similar missions against undesirable regimes elsewhere in the world. Two lessons, to be exact: fact is stranger than fiction; and politics is local. A former employee of the CIA who wished not to be identified was able to confirm the existence of the agency's file for Olive. However, in response to a public information request for files relating to Olive, the CIA's public information officer responded that they could not confirm the existence or nonexistence of files pertaining to Olive at the agency.

Many have searched for Olive Yang like I did, and many fabulists have spun tales about the criminal seductress or power-crazed bandit. But what they may have learned from Olive's true story is that her motivations were more tragic than what they imagined.

Acknowledgments

BIGGEST THANK YOU TO ALICE DAWKINS, DAVID LAWITTS, AND Patrick Winn, for perspective, scholarship, brilliance, and support. I'd like to thank Lin Lei Win, Thin Lei Win, Anasuya Sanyal, Christopher Davy, Robin McDowell, Wowdow Poocharoen, Rosie Cho Cho, Ros Russell, Kelly Macnamara, Kayleigh Long, Blaire Davis, Camille McDorman, Thant Myint-U, and Sofia Busch, Khuensai Jaiyen, John Whalen, Shashank Bengali, Feliz Solomon, Herbert Buchsbaum, Barry Newhouse, Kate Dawson, Daniel Schearf, Lyndal Barry, Samuel Freedman, Christina Brown, Antonia Noori Farzan, especially Matthew Van Meter, Andrea Pitzer, Patricia Elliott, Charmaine Craig, Tali Woodward, Pauline Lee, Philip Bader, Magnus Tulloch, Erin Whittig, and Steve Davis. Thank you for your support and wisdom. Thank you to Joel Bernstein.

To all the people who took risks to speak to me on condition of anonymity, particularly those still in Myanmar today, I thank you here by not naming you.

Thank you Arlene Barlansky and the Library of Congress; thank you to the twelve generous women working at the Myanmar National Archives who helped me; Mia Bruner at the New York Public Library; Larry Ashmun at the University of Wisconsin Library; Cate Brennan at the US National Archives; Alex at the U.N. archive in New York City; Gregory Green at the Cornell University Library. Thank you to the entire Southeast Asia staff at the Australian National Library. Thank you to Stacy Testa, my trusty agent and guiding light.

Thank you to all the very special members of the Yang family who have trusted me with their story. Thank you to Judy Kyi Win, Francis, and Olive Yang, whose passing in 2017 made the world a dimmer place.

Note to Readers

HALF THE CHAPTERS IN THIS BOOK START WITH A COLLECTION OF COM-
monly believed myths about Olive found in other books, which I hope
to debunk. Those passages have been italicized for clarity, so as not to
inadvertently propagate any myths.

Most places in Myanmar, the country formerly known as Burma,
have two names. For the purposes of this book, I have used both historical and contemporary terms for place names where appropriate. For
example, the city of Rangoon in the 1950s is referred to as Yangon in the
twenty-first century.

Olive was assigned female gender at birth and primarily spoke
languages that did not use gendered pronouns. Because the majority of
Olive's relatives used only female pronouns for Olive in English, this
book uses female pronouns for Olive. In Burmese, Olive preferred to
use male-gendered politeness-particles, as was common for women from
Mandalay at the time, and to be addressed as "Uncle," which was not
common for women from any city in Myanmar.

CHAPTER ONE

The Country Formerly Known as Burma

ON A PORCH TUCKED BEHIND A SMALL MAHJONG PARLOR ON THE NORTH side of Yangon, Olive Yang was enjoying a cigarette or two in solitude, with a pot of green tea, watching the relentless evening squall that flooded the driveway to the compound.

Olive was a lifelong insomniac and routinely sat up all night on the porch as old colleagues who passed through town came to pay respects. By morning, Olive was alone and arose to extinguish a final cigarette before retiring. It was July of 2009, in the middle of monsoon season, and when the day dawned, a shattering thunderstorm gradually gave way to spectacular pink and orange skies.

It was so humid that filaments of mold had sprouted across the walls and floor; and while stepping on the glowing butt, Olive suddenly slipped on a slick and mossy, rain-soaked tile and fell hard, backward.

The pain was immense. Olive was unable to get up and called for help.

Initial refusals to see the doctor could not prevent the inevitable diagnosis. Upon returning from the clinic it was clear that the eighty-three-year-old had broken a hip and would require strict bed rest for weeks, maybe months. The caretaker purchased a wheelchair and started giving Olive sponge baths.

Being unable to walk was torturous for someone like Olive, who once boasted the ability to traverse the length of the Salween River's thickly jungled caravan routes faster than any other man on horseback in the Golden Triangle. Now, so much as walking across the courtyard to the mahjong parlor was out of the question, never mind sitting for a game.

Inconsolably cooped-up, with a bum hip that was slow to recover and increasingly cumbersome to care for, Olive's mood plummeted as the weeks wore on. The caretaker learned to open the door slowly whenever he entered the room to clean the bedpan. Olive liked to vent frustration by hurling it his way.

"Moron!" Olive would shout insults at him as he dodged flying filth. "I've been waiting hours!"

So, the caretaker wasn't sure what to expect some weeks later, when he went to Olive's room with a piece of upsetting news: the glorious ceasefire which Olive had negotiated nearly exactly twenty years ago, was broken.

Up in their ancestral homeland, Kokang a few hundred miles north, there had been a violent drug bust. Following a tense standoff, government troops had raided a very heavily guarded weapons and narcotics factory there, fighting their way in with mortars. Clashes were ongoing. It was the end of a prosperous peace that had lasted two decades.

Small pieces of the Yang legacy in the world were disappearing: Olive had ruled that land before. The factory was not far from the family's ancestral gate. Olive knew exactly what spot the troops had attacked; the hills, roads, and strategic approaches there were familiar. The commander of the narcotics facility was Olive's distant cousin.[1] They had forged the historic ceasefire together.

"They're reporting him dead," the caretaker said, worried Olive would be upset. "I know," Olive said, much to the caretaker's surprise, smiling.

Olive had trained that man as a boy; and at one time, even put him in jail, too. Olive knew better than to believe death rumors.

"Well, he was always a bit of a headache, wasn't he?"

The caretaker was surprised to see Olive so nonplussed. Soon enough, he understood why.

Olive was preparing to move to a new home that would be more comfortable given the persistent injury. The day of the move, the caretaker helped Olive into a cotton suit just washed for the occasion—Olive had insisted on style over comfort for the journey. When the entourage arrived to collect their precious passenger, a familiar face emerged from the motorcade, and everybody who was present fell silent.

---

* Peng Jiasheng, leader of the Myanmar National Democratic Alliance Army.

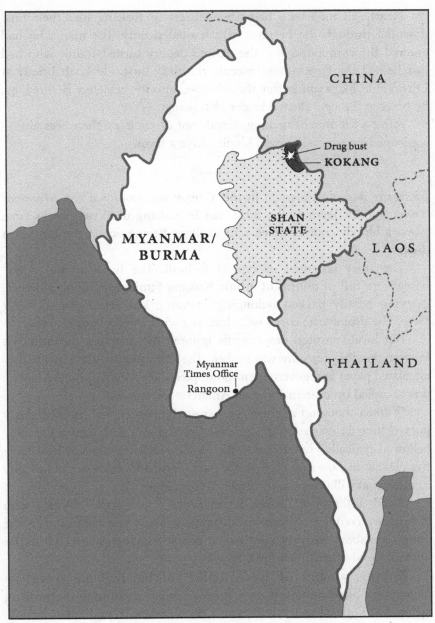

Map 1.1. The location of Kokang, Muse, and the Myanmar Times office, in Myanmar

Nearly all men who had been leaders in Kokang met their final downfall through the betrayal of a trusted deputy. The man who had entered the compound was the trusted deputy-turned-traitor who had just helped the government execute the drug bust. He knelt briefly at Olive's side, like a son, before they climbed into the vehicle.† Before long, he became the new elected leader of Kokang.

After a lifetime of making friends out of enemies, there was always someone in power who owed Uncle Olive a favor.

———

From my desk across town in the Yangon newsroom of the *Myanmar Times*, I didn't learn of the drug bust in Kokang until two weeks later, when a bloody counterattack sent civilians fleeing across the border in droves.[2]

The story emerged in typical fashion. The international news-wires were full of photos of ethnic Kokang families escaping violence, carrying hastily packed belongings, bearing stricken looks on their faces. The diplomatic corps were buzzing with alerts about clashes.

But local censored news media ignored the fact that the country's longest-standing ceasefire was broken. The front page of the most widely circulated paper and government mouthpiece, *The New Light of Myanmar*, was occupied by an item about an Antarctic ice-probe.

"Fifteen thousand refugees flee across the border, and the *Dim Light* puts melting ice on the front page!" A cantankerous editor named Geoffrey bellowed cynically. He referred to the *New Light of Myanmar* by its pejorative nickname, *Dim Light*, which the paper earned for its apparent inability to publish any illuminating or timely information.

Amid a flurry of diplomatic maneuvers to resettle refugees who didn't have complete citizenship documents, there was confusion in the newsroom about whether the Kokang people were considered Myanmar citizens or whether they were Chinese.

Kokang, a strip of land nestled in mountainous gorges in Myanmar's Shan State[3] on the Chinese border, is home to the Kokang ethnic Chinese minority and part of the Golden Triangle, which U.N.

---

† The man's name was Liu Guoxi, and he was the deputy of the purged Peng Jiasheng.

agencies considered among the most productive opium-growing regions in the world.

For each state along Myanmar's borders, there were at least two rebel militias belonging to a variety of ethnic groups with conflicting territorial claims, many derived from a now defunct system of feudal chiefs.

Kokang was the very first rebel-held area to ever negotiate a ceasefire with the Burmese government almost exactly twenty years ago. But, strangely enough, in the decades since it had been agreed upon, the signatories claimed, the papers had never been properly signed.[4]

Our stories about it were cut by censors for nearly a month, until the counterattack was quelled, when the *Dim Light*'s headline read, "Government recognizes cooperation for development of Kokang Region."

I was baffled by the phrase "recognizes cooperation." Something like "Kokang army defeated" would have been more direct.

The next line continued with a prescriptive assurance that the people were "much pleased with it," and in the years since the ceasefire, Kokang had developed far more than in the past. "Artless" purged rebels were encouraged to abandon their ethnic leaders, turn themselves over, cooperate with the Myanmar military, and return to the "legal fold," as if they were errant sheep lost in the hills, searching for home.

Shocking, gory photos of Myanmar soldiers who had been executed at point blank range with their jaws blown off and carnage dripping from their faces, unlike anything I had ever seen in a familiar newspaper, filled the back pages. Among the grievous crimes prominently noted to shame rebels: distributing native Chinese-language textbooks in schools.

Kokang was now firmly under the control of the Myanmar military perhaps for the first time in history, serving as a warning to other rebel groups—all as a result of this drug bust.

The Myanmar military commander, Min Aung Hlaing, who led the operation received accolades upon successfully taking control of Kokang and eliminating what was then seen as one of the greatest military threats on the country's border. As a result, he was promoted to the rank of general.[5]

Nobody in the newsroom seemed to be able to point to a defined beginning of the conflict. According to the *Dim Light*, however, the root causes were threefold: (1) events of the colonial era, (2) CIA forces who got deeply involved in large-scale smuggling of narcotic drugs, and (3) overwhelming selfishness.

It sounded like conspiracy theories, if not quaintly judgmental.

That year, in 2009, I had moved halfway across the world to Myanmar a month before, shortly after graduating with a degree in Chinese from Washington University in Saint Louis, Missouri. A friend mentioned the *Myanmar Times* was hiring a sub-editor, presenting it as a unique opportunity to work as a journalist in one of the world's last remaining military dictatorships. It would offer a rare glimpse into a hermetic country that had endured decades of conflict and oppression but had emerged on the cusp of what the world saw as a stunning transformation to democracy.

For a young person who still believed in the unassailable virtues of international humanitarian aid and a vegetarian diet, it was perfect.

When I arrived in Yangon, the city felt suspended in time. The taxis at the airport were automotive relics. Mobile phones were rare. The monsoon-soaked city looked like it was losing a battle against the jungle. Sarong-clad men lurched across broken sidewalks; children selling jasmine garlands darted between the cars. The *Myanmar Times* newsroom was in a brick warehouse building with a prominent sign just beyond a gilded bridge on a swampy corner of downtown with a street-side tea shop out front.

The first day of work I signed up for the uniquely exasperating responsibility of censorship duty. My initial excitement soon gave way to great frustration. The military's side of the story prevailed. While certain narratives were favored, some were left completely untold, effectively eliminating entire facets of society. Sometimes it was simply due to timing: our newspaper was issued weekly partially because there weren't enough English-reading censors to be able to keep up with a daily schedule.

The newspaper's censorship liaison was a slight man who ferried proofs back and forth from the censorship office and was easily startled. Though it was his job to bargain on behalf of the stories, it was hard to imagine him being very hard-nosed with the censors.

The censors worked in a building that had once served as a torture chamber for the Japanese secret police during World War II. People joked they were now torturing writing, and that where they had previously cut people to extract military intelligence, they were now cutting words or ideas. So, it was nicknamed the "literary torture" office.[6]

Stories were submitted for literary torture on Thursdays and Fridays, and Saturday nights our proofs came back with cuts. Each week, we hoped enough uncensored copy would return to fill a whole paper, and it was our job, by law, to make sure whatever remained still made sense without conspicuous gaps. It was against the law for the paper to go out full of holes, or as Geoffrey said, "looking like Swiss cheese."

"How do they decide what to cut?" I asked a colleague.

"Beats me. A lot of it is things you'd expect, but sometimes it's inexplicable or silly," he said, pointing to the page in front of him with a photo of a woman whose dress had been photoshopped to be less revealing. "Last month they cut a foreboding horoscope. You have to imagine the censors didn't want to be responsible for delivering bad news to somebody important."

Of course, criticisms of the military were banned. When I wrote a full-page story about the winner of the annual nationwide transgender beauty contest, it came back from the censors circled in red, with two large, red crosses emphatically cutting the words and the image. Nobel laureate Aung San Suu Kyi, symbol of democracy, beacon of hope, was so unmentionable, even in casual conversation she was referred to obliquely as "The Lady."

In the foreign media, dictator Senior General Than Shwe was portrayed as the reviled Beast to Suu Kyi's Beauty: out of touch, authoritarian, paranoid, and brutal. But in our paper, any news or pictures of Than Shwe, no matter how small, went on the front page, where no other image was allowed to appear higher than his. His more unsavory deeds, however, did not appear in our pages: such as the brutal crackdown he ordered that left monks dead during the uprising in 2007. The thousands of people who died in the uprising and coup that preceded his rise to power were not discussed.

There hadn't really been uncensored newspapers in Myanmar since the military coup in the sixties. The *Myanmar Times* publisher, a bald-headed, ruddy-faced Australian,[7] bragged that he had smuggled the mint-green printing presses in from New Zealand in 1999, right under the junta's nose. Back then, when the paper first started printing, it was illegal to own something as innocuous as a photocopying machine. His first Burmese business partner had been in jail on retroactive censorship charges for the last five years. He liked to think of himself as a subversive thorn in the side of a repressive government; his critics saw him as an opportunistic apologist who published government propaganda.

The publisher kept a framed photo of himself at a drug-burning ceremony in Shan State on a shelf in his office. In the photo, blocks of heroin were stacked neatly alongside methamphetamines under a festive display with ribbons.[8] The piles looked like they were being presented at an elementary school science project. He grinned gleefully in the picture, posing for the camera in front of the piles about to be set alight in a raging bonfire, holding a packet wrapped in brown paper in his hand.

The government made a big media event out of setting seized drugs on fire in Shan State, where the publisher explained all the "best" narcotics in the country came from. Journalists and diplomats were flown out to observe, to make a show out of cracking down on narcotics producers, in the hopes the photos would make it into the press.

He pointed to the brown paper-wrapped packets in the photo with a knowing look. "That's some good stuff, too. Top quality No. 4, China White."

That fluffy white powder—the most potent, injectable form of heroin—had been seized on the road from Kokang. It was derived from morphine produced in poppy fields controlled by generals who had once answered to Olive. But I did not know that yet. A coworker later told me the publisher had returned from the drug burning ceremony with a brown paper packet stuffed in his carry-on, which had eventually made its way to a staff party. He assured me that the heroin had indeed been of top quality.

"They love to make a spectacle of their counter-narcotics operations, but they're all benefiting from it. That is why the military will never lose its grip on power," the publisher told me brashly, referring to the Burmese generals in the photo.

The Burmese military pitted rebels against one another in competition for control of lucrative resource concessions like teak, jade, and also illicit narcotics. Rebel armies who signed ceasefire agreements with the government enriched the generals who turned a blind eye to their illicit trade and then cracked down on them when it was convenient.

"Everybody's in on it: military, rebels, even the CIA," the publisher said.

I was skeptical. Perhaps he was a fan of the Mel Gibson comedy *Air America*, about pilots in Vietnam who discover they're being used as cover by the CIA to traffic opium. He sounded like the *Dim Light*.

What I did not know at the time: the *Dim Light* was right. The roots of the dispute in Kokang were indeed events of the colonial era; and CIA forces did, in fact, get deeply involved in the narcotics trade. And many believed that Kokang has been cursed with upheaval, ever since the indomitable Olive Yang got carried away with overwhelming selfishness.

The drab pages of the *Dim Light* proclaimed on a daily basis that the Union was well on its way to transitioning from a military dictatorship to a "discipline-flourishing democracy." Senior General Than Shwe intended to allow the Union to elect its first civilian government in five decades and retire.

"'Discipline-flourishing' means 'military-controlled,'" Geoffrey told me one day. "Than Shwe knows what they do to dictators, and he doesn't want to die in jail."

When the anticipated historic election finally arrived in November of 2010, I took an assignment with Voice of America because their shortwave radio news broadcasts were uncensored.

The broadcasts were regarded by the government as so threatening, there was a daily feature in the *Dim Light* denouncing Voice of America as foreign meddling, in a small box that read like Orwellian poetry:

"VOA airing skyful of lies! Saboteurs watch your step! The public be warned of killers in the air waves!"

It was slightly puzzling, if not insulting to a well-meaning reporter like me, to be accused of sabotage or be constantly asked if Voice of America was a cover organization for the CIA.

But I was so eager to work for an uncensored news outlet, I thought nothing of it; so I passed the State Department contractor background check and published under a pseudonym to avoid being blacklisted.

By the end of the election, it was like a spell had been broken. Senior General Than Shwe retired as planned, and his handpicked successors were elected with a resounding majority. The unmentionable Aung San Suu Kyi was released. Other political prisoners were granted amnesty, and even the censorship office closed. But nothing was quite what it seemed. Journalists were silenced with bogus lawsuits. New dissidents were jailed. What started as riots in the Northwest turned into a genocide of ethnic Rohingya Muslims before our eyes, and the military helped perpetrate it.

Olive, meanwhile, was enjoying a new home, surrounded by soldiers and a young, attractive Chinese nurse with long, silky hair. The militia headquarters several hundred miles north near the Chinese border wasn't Olive's ancestral home, but this was the safest possible place for Olive to be. Kokang was still crawling with mercenaries. Every afternoon, though still in an apparently frail state, Olive watched the troops rally in formation on their porch, giving orders from a wheelchair.

Figure 1.1. Olive smiling at her home in June 2015.
GABRIELLE PALUCH.

It wasn't until 2015, when the Kokang rebel militia that was purged my first month at the *Myanmar Times* came back for vengeance, that I first heard of Olive.

That's when Olive's purged distant cousin staged the deadliest attack on the Myanmar military in recent history, recapturing the territory from which he'd been chased years prior, in a last-ditch effort to force his way into the peace process. Some ethnic groups had already signed agreements when a wave of one thousand Kokang rebels caught the Myanmar military in their old garrisons by surprise.

Nearly eight hundred government troops had already died by the time I attended a public ceremony for the signing of a historic nationwide ceasefire that March.

The agreement was to include every single rebel group; a peace agreement to end all civil wars in Myanmar that had been raging more or less uninterrupted since the country had gained independence.[9] Kokang rebels were still engaged in battle with the army as the pen hit the paper on the peace agreement.

In the press gaggle, I asked the government negotiator if he expected to make peace with Kokang rebels.

"Those Kokang are actually an illegal renegade group. They are Chinese, not Myanmar," a negotiator told us, describing the Kokang rebel army as a Beijing-funded drug-trafficking militia, with an irrelevant claim to power.

"Are they not entitled to Myanmar citizenship?" I asked.

"Not exactly," he claimed, "besides, their ceasefire expired."

Ah yes, I thought, the old handshake-ceasefire that had crumbled during my first month at the *Myanmar Times*. Another journalist suggested to me that "Miss Hairy Legs" might know something about the ceasefire's terms. Miss Hairy Legs had apparently acted as a silent broker.

Miss Hairy Legs was an extremely perplexing name. It was unusual for someone in Myanmar to have such a descriptive moniker—and frankly, unusual for women to have hairy legs. Miss Hairy Legs, or Olive Yang, was mentioned fleetingly in a smattering of books that alluded to her domination of the opium trade with a small personal army named "Olive's Boys" who eventually staged a coup against her feudal chieftain brother. She was repeatedly described as having taken a gun to school in her backpack, had a tendency to dress like a man, and had a high-profile lesbian affair with a famous movie star. And in one account, she was alleged to have cooperated with the CIA.

I had never before heard of a military leader in Myanmar, rebel or otherwise, openly admitting to being a lesbian. It was surprising to hear that a woman, much less a cross-dressing one, had been at the table for the very first peace deal the government had signed with a rebel army whose name was never mentioned—even though there was a time when Miss Hairy Legs was infamous.

There was a plethora of infamous characters that swirled around the Golden Triangle whose real lives had inspired fiction scattered across novels and legends.

There was the American Baptist missionary William Young, who came to proselytize hill tribespeople in the nineteenth century, baptized in remarkable numbers, delivering entire villages from their primitive ways. His sons and grandsons eventually became US intelligence assets during World War II and beyond, inspiring volumes of spy pulp throughout the Cold War.[10]

Or the covert paramilitary operative Tony Poe who became infamous for keeping the pickled heads of communist guerilla leaders he killed in jars. He swore to have inspired the Colonel Kurtz character in the film *Apocalypse Now* and rescued the Dalai Lama from execution—both were exaggerated claims that were only partially true.

There had even been a beauty-queen rebel-leader, Louisa Benson, crowned "Miss Burma" before leading her deceased husband's militia on the border in the 1960s.

Since my first day of skepticism in the publisher's office at the *Myanmar Times*, I had learned one of the first eyebrow-raising failures of covert US foreign policy executed by the newly formed CIA during the Cold War involved arming and financing anti-communist Chinese troops in exchange for opium, firmly lodging them in Burmese borderlands as a military threat for decades.[11]

CIA-supported anti-communist guerilla armies provided the intelligence-gathering and logistics basis for clandestine operations throughout the Cold War, including ethnic minority rebel mercenaries in the secret war in Laos against the North Vietnamese.[12] Much to my dismay, I had learned the transmitters that were used for the radio stories I did for Voice of America were stationed in old Cold War–era CIA facilities that had been logistics hubs to support those missions and were even used as torture blacksite facilities.

By the early 1970s, millions of dollars worth of heroin seized in New York City had originated from their enterprises. Networks once supported by the CIA were eventually blamed by US Congress for supplying the heroin epidemic. That is how so many legendary opium warlords from Shan State rumored to be cooperating with the CIA, came to be counterintuitively condemned by drug enforcement agencies.

The most infamous among them, the "Godfather of Heroin," Lo Hsing Han, once sentenced to death for his crimes but celebrated by hundreds as a hero at his funeral. Not to be confused of course with the "King of Opium" Khun Sa. Between the two of them, they supplied almost half of the heroin consumed worldwide for over a decade, leading to indictments by drug enforcement officials in federal court in Brooklyn.[13]

It was wild but plausible that "Miss Hairy Legs" was swept up in missions designed to set the foundation for US hegemony in the twentieth century through covert CIA narcotics-funded operations, in the same crucible as the architects of the Cold War.

But for every story about Olive Yang, there was an opposite one that seemed like it could also be true. One account claimed she was illiterate, and yet apparently, she had been a teacher. She was either a folk hero or a murderous bandit. Either a fearsome dragon-lady with great riches and land to her name or a poverty-stricken widow. A champion of democracy or a dictator. Pioneer or mental patient. There were so many conflicting details about Miss Hairy Legs that they couldn't all be true. It seemed like people were willing to believe anything about her.

Olive's life and identity defied every Burmese social norm and sounded more like the opium-slinging antiheroes draped across the covers of the raunchy spy novels that littered Yangon's downtown bookshops.

At first, I encountered a broad canon of death rumors. For every different name by which she was known—Olive Yang, Miss Hairy Legs, Number Two, Two-Gun Mulan, the Kokang chieftain's sister—she appeared to have died in a different way.

There were those who swore she was killed at the hands of, curiously enough, the infamous Godfather of Heroin himself, Lo Hsing Han, who allegedly owed his success to Olive's patronage.

Some told me the infamous drug lord of the Golden Triangle, the "double-gun old lady," was executed for heroin trafficking in China.

Another journalist told me he had given up his search for the legendary figure, because he'd heard she had supposedly died in Yangon in the infamous Insein Prison. But Olive's name didn't appear in any of the records of known deceased political prisoners. So when I then heard the rumor that she had died in an insane asylum, I concluded the confusion must have arisen out of a foreigner's misunderstanding of the name of Insein Prison.

The belief Olive was dead was so widespread that I started to look for graves. But there was no obituary for her anywhere—not in English, Burmese, or Chinese.

It seemed like a great oversight, that at the beginning of the interminable narcotics war was a gender-queer opium kingpin of noble descent and secret broker of a peace deal nobody had ever inquired about. Surely the story of how the Yang family came to be in Myanmar and gained noble status was important to answering the question as to whether or not Kokang people should be considered part of Myanmar or China and why the conflict in Kokang was happening in the first place.

My questions about Olive's supposed exploits quickly filled several pages, recalling the *Dim Light*'s condemnation of CIA forces and "overwhelming selfishness" I had read about my first week in Myanmar.

Was it possible the extraordinary stories about the legendary CIA asset and folk hero were true? I resolved to find Olive, armed with a list of details that I hoped she could verify, starting at the very beginning, with the family's ancestral origins, and the *Dim Light*'s story about events of the colonial era.

CHAPTER TWO

Before There Was a Golden Triangle

THE MORE FANCIFUL RELATIVES SAY LITTLE ROUND-FACED OLIVE EMERGED from toddlerhood already a confident, boyish gunslinger with a penchant for smoking tobacco—and an utter terror to her mother. They even say Olive tried to shoot her mother when she came to bind her feet.

The family guard became Olive's favorite companions from an early age, and she easily learned any skills they could impart to her. Almost as soon as she had learned to walk, she learned to ride. With the crack of her whip she could pilot a pony so swiftly as to outpace any of her father's levies up the steepest of Kokang's hills. And almost as soon as she could talk, she could aim a pistol with such uncanny accuracy as to strike fear into the hearts of grown men; and could smoke a cigarette while doing knife tricks before she could read or write.

Olive's mother, on the other hand, had been a child bride of exceptional beauty with tiny, bound feet, who daintily rode her horse side-saddle. Because she wanted her daughter to grow up to be a desirable marriage prospect, she prepared to inflict the same terrifyingly gory tradition she had suffered stoically as a young girl.

Olive knew she didn't want tiny feet that made it hard to walk. She didn't want to ride side-saddle. Olive wanted to keep riding forwards as she already did, just like her brothers.

When the dreaded day arrived for Olive's binding, her mother steeled herself for what she suspected would be a battle.

As some tell the story, Olive was ready when they came for her with the bandages. There was shrieking from the chambers as nursemaids ran out into the yard, her mother trailing not far behind. When Olive finally emerged, there was a pistol in her hands, and a cigarette dangling from her lips. "I need my feet for riding," she said, as she raised her gun.

Olive was different from her sisters, difficult to control from the very beginning. Not even her father, the chieftain, could tell her what to do.

So, when a few years later, the story about Olive shooting a classmate at the Guardian Angel's Convent school spread around, it was hardly surprising to those who knew her well. The precipitating details of the event all got lost in the telling of it, and Olive had used language so creatively foul, the nuns had refused to repeat it. But one message remained certain. Don't cross Olive Yang, she carries a pistol and isn't afraid to use it, not even in a convent.

And some others, who knew Olive even less intimately, said her more diabolical ways started in childhood. Her nobleman father had spoiled her rotten, fulfilling her every demand from a young age. She was even allowed to order guardsmen to beat servants for personal amusement, devising new ways to torture them as a game. And by the age of twelve, she had become so impishly willful, she ordered the hands of a clumsy servant chopped off, just because it pleased her.[1]

When Olive was born, everybody called her Erjie, meaning "second sister" in Chinese, because every child in their family called one another by names that indicated their gender and birth order. Though her parents chose an auspicious given name for their new daughter, Yang Jin Xiu, wherever she went, people called her Erjie. She was reminded she was just a girl and came second.[2] In their traditional Chinese household, three generations lived under one roof, and the women ate after the men.

They were a big family attended by dozens of servants who lived in a stone court with a white perimeter fortress wall, painstakingly built atop a small hill with a steep set of one hundred stairs. Erjie was a restless baby, always going missing among the quince and cherry tree orchards in the courtyards. So, while her five older siblings all slept in their own beds with nursemaids, her parents made her sleep between them in their bed so she wouldn't crawl out and wander off during the night.

Figure 2.1. The Yang family tree.
KATHLEEN MCLEOD.

The year of Olive's birth in 1927, the murderous bandit Sanhpe, infamously known as the "Robin Hood of Burma," miraculously evaded a prolonged bounty-hunt in the jungle by 1,000 sepoys that succeeded in turning up only a diary detailing his crimes. As a judge signed his execution warrant, those who believed he possessed the supernatural powers of invisibility, and immunity to bullets conveyed upon him by his magical tattoos, would not believe he was truly dead.[3]

Born the second daughter to a hereditary ruler, it was never Erjie's fate to be a leader. But that year, 1927, internecine bickering was to portend an evil omen as Erjie's father came to power. It set in motion the demise of the Yang dynasty—as well as the fulfillment of a family curse that loomed over their destinies. And, some believed, gave rise to the reincarnation of Burma's new Robin Hood.

Whenever Yang rulers made important decisions, they traditionally sought the advice of an old geomancer and snake oil salesman, who descended from his secluded hut with his chicken bones and divination coins on bazaar days. Before Erjie's grandfather died, he learned of a grim yet vague prediction. The geomancer told him his hexagrams had aligned to indicate the Yang family dynasty's days would be numbered after the eighth generation—in other words, Erjie's generation.

The day Erjie's grandfather passed, their mourning father was summoned by his overlord who threatened to remove him from power, because a rival pretender-cousin claimed his bloodline were the rightful rulers of Kokang.

The pretender was the son of Erjie's one-eyed great-granduncle, their extraordinary ancestor who had sacrificed an eye to an exploding powder flask during battle.[4] His glorious decades-long reign was as regent in place of his brother, who also died an untimely death. On his deathbed, the one-eyed great-granduncle kept his vow to his deceased brother and chose his nephew—Erjie's grandfather—as his successor. But after Erjie's grandfather assumed duties his jealous cousins believed should have been theirs, they plotted against him. Their overlord, Sao Hom Hpa, obliged and supported the pretenders against Erjie's father.

Erjie's father prevailed after appealing to the British governor in Rangoon, seized his rival cousin's property and sent him into exile with a co-conspirator, never to return.[5] But just a few months later, a calamity befell the family.

Erjie's father had accompanied his firstborn son on the days-long journey to Lashio where he was supposed to be the first Yang to attend English school. But after sharing a meal with relatives-in-law the evening they arrived, Erjie's first brother fell mysteriously ill with what appeared to be food poisoning the night before he was supposed to begin his first day of school.[6] Erjie's brother didn't respond to the usual home remedy of opium; within two days, he was dead at the age of ten, leaving his duty to the family line unfulfilled. Their father set out the next day with his firstborn heir's corpse to return home to his wife and remaining children.

Their mother was particularly stricken. Because her son was the only person to have fallen ill after the meal they ate, she suspected it had been a retaliatory poisoning, avenging the exiled cousin.[7] Among the irretrievable losses her first son's death inflicted was the interruption of their noble bloodline. Out of grief and suspicion, she banished their entire branch of the family, which coincidentally included her sister.[8]

The geomancer's prophecy loomed over the remaining children of the cursed eighth generation. Erjie's father's resentment grew for Sao Hom Hpa, their threatening overlord who had nearly removed him from power; but he developed an affection for the British rulers who protected him.

Perched high above the more tempestuous monsoons of Burma's central plains, there isn't a flat square mile in all of Kokang, which makes growing rice virtually impossible. But what's bad for the paddy is good for the poppy: with a drier climate and sandier soil, Kokang is an opium grower's dream. The flowers determined the rhythms of their lives and provided for everything they needed.[9]

From the hives they kept for the bees that pollinated their fields, they harvested particularly prized honey with a flavor unique to Kokang. During the lunar new year, they ate poppy seed buns sweetened with poppy-scented honey.

There were no moral strictures against smoking opium. At the time, the Kokang attitude toward the opium from their poppy fields was akin to the Frenchman's attitude to his wine from the grapes in his vineyard. In the evenings after dinner, Erjie's father sometimes filled his pipe with gummy opium that his wife would cook over their stove. The earthy fragrance filled their house as it boiled in the kitchen, a thick and soothing cloud the children associated with home.

Any villager who grew poppies in Kokang was required to give one-fifth of the raw opium they brought to market as taxes to the Yang rulers, the sole legal wholesale agents. Subjects who came to the family court to pay taxes kowtowed at the ruler's feet and the shrines to his ancestors.[10]

To export opium, merchants required the stamp of the Yang family's imperial copper seal of the Qing court.[11] They were received by armed family guards in red turbans, and passed under the arched gate adorned with a poetic couplet written by Erjie's grandfather. It read: "It is a shame to earn riches, without good strategies."[12]

Erjie learned the stories of their ancestors from a young age. The first Yang ancestor was a general who came to Yunnan in the entourage of the last scion of the Ming dynasty and who was deposed and strangled with a bowstring. The Yang ancestor settled down and became a tea merchant. His grandson was erroneously presumed ruler of a cluster of remote villages between craggy hills, after coincidentally saving them from attacking bandits. He gained the trust of the chieftain who was too elderly to reach the villages,[13] began collecting taxes, and vowed to forevermore serve a duty of guardianship to his people through a line of firstborn sons in 1739. That is how the Yang family became rulers.[14]

He buried his parents in a spot on a hill deemed appropriate according to Daoist customs on the very northern tip of his land in Red Rock River. Gradually, more and more villages sought the Yang family's protection. Across three centuries, subsequent generations of an unbroken line of hereditary rulers of Yang sons who served as guardians of the frontier between Burma and China were entombed in different parts as their land grew over the years.[15]

The land's original inhabitants were not Chinese. They were a hill tribe who spoke their own language, worshiped the animal spirits of the mountains and streams, and were known as the Hke Hpok people. Their language had no script, and though they did not know from whence they originally came, they believed their ancestors were nine little ogrelets born of the seeds of a magical gourd.[16]

Until Erjie's one-eyed great-granduncle received a swashbuckling colonial officer named Sir James George Scott in his court, Kokang had been part of China. But after British troops deposed the Burmese King, Scott was tasked with clarifying British Burma's borders and pacifying its people.*

In a reclining chair sharing his opium pipe, Scott was duly impressed by the nearly blinded Yang ruler's mettle, who did not seem subdued by his injured eye. Scott saw value in Kokang's opium-specked hills: he began to build a garrison, promised a British-built railway, and negotiated a triumphant trade with Beijing, who officially ceded Kokang in 1897. Because Kokang's impassable gorges to the east made it difficult to reach from within Burma, they were made vassals of the neighboring chieftain's state.[17] That is how the Yang family's land came to belong to British Burma, though it was too remote to come under the Crown's firm ruling grasp.

The responsibilities the Yangs inherited along with their family name anchored them to the special resting place of their ancestors' graves—not the British Empire to the west or the Chinese emperor to the east. Erjie's would be the eighth generation of the ruling family to rest there, and their nobility came with an obligation to help and protect their people, just as their ancestor had done in the face of attacking bandits.

Once, during a banquet for all the headmen at the family court—Erjie couldn't have been more than four or five years old according to the siblings—she nearly accidentally shot one of them. Curious Erjie had wandered into the courtyard and was admiring a pistol that had been

---

* British opium traders first arrived in the port of Rangoon in 1824. After forcing Imperial China and the Kingdom of Siam to legalize opium, Kokang's opium fields were sandwiched between producers and customers. The first British envoys came bearing gifts of wool uniforms in 1889 and occupied Kokang with 75 soldiers in barracks known as "foreigner's garrison." Kokang muleteers were handsomely rewarded with high salaries when repeated expeditions were required to convince rulers unwilling to submit to the Crown. Scott referred to the Kokang people as "Chinamen." They were predominantly ethnically Han, spoke a Mandarin dialect similar to the one spoken by members of the Ming court from Nanjing, and practiced Chinese religious rituals.

set down by one of the attendees while they weren't looking and started holding it just like she'd seen the guardsmen do.

Suddenly, a shot rang out, a bullet very narrowly missed one of the assembled elders, and all the village headmen including Erjie's father ducked and cowered for cover. Little Erjie, still holding the weapon, responded to the frightened men by laughing. It instantly earned Erjie a reputation for fearlessness among all the headmen in Kokang.

Their father took note of his daughter's nerve and courage and gave Erjie a pistol and a particularly hearty, small white pony, bred from majestic Yunnanese horses. Erjie was assigned an entourage with muleteer-guardsmen and flag-bearers to travel with her, like all members of the family. Erjie easily learned to ride the steep trails that twisted like sheep intestines up the poppy-specked hills under the watchful eyes of their guardsmen. Ordinary travelers dismounted and bowed as a sign of respect when they encountered them on the trails.

Every year in October the cloudy skies of the rainy season gave way to brighter, sunnier days, and Kokang's terraced hillside fields transformed with an annual spectacle of blossoming poppies in a spectrum of crimson hues from deep purple to variegated pink and white as far as the eye could see.

In the spring after the second harvest, the main temple in Old Street Village was surrounded by an opium market that lasted over a week, sometimes two.[18] It was Erjie's favorite time of year, when all manner of tribespeople and traders from far and wide came with all manner of goods.

Kokang's best opium came from the fields of the only two remaining villages of Hke Hpok people, who were no longer as numerous as the Chinese merchants who had become their rulers. Everybody in Kokang liked the kind old geomancer and snake oil salesman, who came to sell dried animal turds and bones, attracting crowds when he extolled the virtues of his wares.[19]

"This mass of excretory treasure from only the rarest of miscellaneous animals deserves an exorbitant price!" He would bleat, pointing at the mounds on his blankets with his cane, before launching into the Yunnanese folk songs that recited the tales of their ancestors.

Then there were the Wa headhunters, who rarely left their villages except to come to market to trade opium for salt. Like the Hke Hpok, the Wa, too, were hill people who said they came from the seeds of a prolific gourd. Though the Wa were notoriously gullible, no man at the market who was fond of his head dared cheat them.

One time, nobody could say when, a Wa woman bought bad rice seeds that would not sprout from a Chinese trader who cheated her. She went to see her witch-doctor, who instructed the villagers to kill the Chinese and use their heads as an offering. They did as instructed, and the harvest was bountiful that year. That is why every year, they spilled blood from human sacrifices on their soil before planting rice and kept the decapitated heads on spikes outside their stockaded villages to warn outsiders to stay away.[20]

There was a time when many of the hill people lived in the valleys. The Wa once had knowledge of the written word and built a great civilization that spanned as far as the sea and produced the finest silver. Whatever happened to make them flee must have been terrible and a very long time ago, because nobody could remember. Now the Wa mostly lived in stockaded villages, in a wide area just south of Kokang, around Savage Mountain, and were suspicious of the Chinese.[21]

When Erjie's one-eyed great-granduncle was ruler, British officers with foolish ambitions to trace the border between China and British Burma came to the Wa states. They had heard fabulous tales of treasures in the Wa hills, like one about a golden deer who entered a cave and never came out. Most Wa had never seen white men before and didn't allow them to enter the cave lest they disturb its spirits.

Many years before, the Wa chieftain of Banhong had allowed the Chinese emperor to mine their silver, with the understanding they would pay half the mined bullion in taxes. Tens of thousands of conscripts were banished to work there, it became the most productive silver mine in all the land, and the Chinese appointed him as the king of Savage Mountain. But when the Chinese workers tried to smuggle silver out in a coffin, the Wa grew suspicious because it took sixteen men to carry it. Each last one was slaughtered. The mine was shut down, and the chiefs made a pact not to allow outsiders into their mines.[22]

When the British came to demarcate the border on Savage Mountain near the mine, Chinese neighbors started rumors in Wa villages that if they allowed white men to tread their soil, their rivers would dry up. It caused such great panic, that the Chinese border commissioner agreed to offer up two of his soldiers as human sacrifices to appease them. Fifty frenzied chanting Was were liquored up and readied for the scheduled beheading ritual, when a delegation of British officers coincidentally visited the public marketplace, accompanied by ten Chinese officers who decided to join.

The drunken Was, with a crowd of four hundred behind them, shot at them with crossbows and muzzle-loading guns, before stoning them all the way out of town. They decapitated several officers, including some Chinese ones but marveled at the quality of the two British ones. The chieftain made it known that the British ones were particularly desirable as they retained their virtue and benevolent powers for well beyond ten years.[23] British reinforcements arrived to avenge the murders, burning twelve villages. The Chinese believed one of the British officers had started the violence by stealing a pomelo. The British said the Wa hated the Chinese so much, they spontaneously started killing whenever they saw them.[24]

After that, Scott decided rather than risk decapitation, he would leave the border undemarcated where the wild Wa still practiced head-hunting. That is why there were no more boundary pillars built on Savage Mountain, and the border was left undecided south of Kokang.

Just north of Kokang, in the mountainous plains of Burma's Kachin State, the borders were also left undecided. More British officers trying to tame wild hill people died in similar incidents following the Kachin Troubles of 1893. There was a time when Kokang had many Kachin people, but Erjie's grandfather drove rebellious Kachins out from Kokang across the Salween in his first battle as a young man. Since then, the Kachin were so hated in Kokang, they knew they entered the Yang family's land on pain of death. The British superintendent at the time agreed it was a good decision to banish them, because the Kachins were rotten subjects and terrible neighbors. Now, their descendants all lived on the land of Sao Hom Hpa, their odious overlord.[25]

Most white men who ventured into the Shan hills did not fare well, but an elderly American Baptist missionary of unwavering faith named William Marcus Young repeatedly defied death to gain tens of thousands adherents among the people of the hills.

Among the Lahu hill people, a tribe of skilled big-game hunters, he fulfilled a widespread legend that when a man from across the blue sea came bearing a white book, he would restore to them the long-lost knowledge of the written word. True to the legend, the Youngs developed a written script for their language to translate the bible.

One day, William rode into a stockaded village in a district of a formidable headhunting Wa priest, hoping to spread the gospel. He was with his son, Harold, who was armed with a rifle. Loinclothed Wa warriors gathered to defend themselves from the intruders and launched a stone at them. But it missed, injuring another Wa, instead. Then, their rifles jammed. Believing this was an omen, their village's witch-doctor and priest suddenly signaled to the warriors to lay down their arms.

The priest of that Wa village had heard of the legend of the white prophet and believed they were to abandon their headhunting ways. He asked to be baptized by the Youngs and began to preach the gospel to other Wa religious leaders who slowly gave up the practice of headhunting.

The Youngs developed a Wa script, published a bible, and founded schools. After many of the villagers were baptized, they bequeathed to Harold the magical iron staff once carried by witch-doctors to bless the raids for the human sacrifices and ritual beheadings they had chosen to give up. The staff bore with it great powers of protection from evil, imparted to it by its use of one of the last great Wa religious leaders. That is how some Wa people came to follow Jesus and regard the Youngs as kinds of deities, too.[26]

The Youngs were pious, hardworking, and widely respected—except Harold, who had a reputation as an incorrigible womanizer with a predilection for the fair-skinned Lahu women. Shortly after his first son was born at their new mission in China, he was accused of violating a Lahu woman's honor and was banished.

When Erjie turned six, their mother began with the incessant reminders to behave like a girl and insisted it was time to bind her feet. The practice

25

had been officially banned by the Chinese government for over ten years. But their mother, who married at age fourteen and never learned to read, had three-inch feet and believed the procedure was required of a more elegant woman. Besides, they could afford to do it, and it would serve to pacify her fearless, headstrong little daughter, who was so difficult to control.

Erjie had seen the gruesome dressings on her older sister's feet; and witnessed the horrifying, wincing pain and difficulty her sister experienced walking afterward. Erjie was heartbroken to learn she would soon be effectively homebound: almost as soon as she had learned the joy of riding, it would be taken away.

Nursemaids were called upon; Erjie kicked and screamed as they chased her around the family court with a mallet until she was finally held down. They broke her feet and crushed her bones, folded her toes down, and bandaged them. They gave her opium to alleviate the pain. Ordinarily, a monthslong process of tightening layers of bandages would have followed. Erjie's resistance was less dramatic but no less heroic than the more exaggerated stories people told about gunpoint threats.

Even with constant supervision, Erjie would not be subdued and managed to find ways to unbind her feet. Nevertheless, by the time her parents relented out of frustration, Erjie's feet were already badly broken. They remained remarkably small and deformed even after healing, and Erjie was forced to relearn to walk on her heels.

But by the time her two younger sisters came of age, their parents no longer believed the ritual was necessary, and Erjie's younger sisters knew her headstrong resistance had gone a long way to convincing their mother it was cruel and unnecessary. So Erijie was the last of the Yang daughters to have her feet mutilated, and they regarded her as the savior of their feet.[27]

That year, British troops who built a road to Savage Mountain besieged the silver mine's furnace room of the Wa chieftain of Banhong. The tribes of seventeen Wa chieftains banded together for a battle that lasted four months and killed many. Nobody in Kokang dared travel south, lest they wander into their warpath, and Erjie's father helped the British subdue the unrest by sending two thousand mules.

When the Wa made war, their witch-doctors presided over rituals to bless their raids. They would sprinkle a small line of raw rice and burn incense in an auspicious spot for the blessed ambush, where they would hide in the thick bushes. Kokang muleteers who survived the dangers that lurked on Savage Mountain returned with great riches and warned the children of the Wa witch-doctors lines of raw rice on the trails, so Erjie knew to listen for the clicking of their tongues that signaled their attacks.[28]

When Erjie was ten, she set out from home for a four-day journey to Lashio with an armed horseback escort to attend her first day at school. Though it was just one hundred miles away, the prospect of traveling to a new town was a great adventure because it meant crossing the Salween River for the first time. Their mother believed that to travel west of the Salween River that formed Kokang's western border was to meet certain death.[29]

At the crossing where the river carved deep, dramatic gorges, Erjie kowtowed three times before climbing aboard the hollowed-out tree which served as a ferry. Erjie had never learned to swim, so her mother instructed her to toss coins into the river to appease the river spirits and avoid drowning.[30]

At the Catholic Guardian Angel's Convent School in Lashio, run by nuns of the Pontifical Institute in Milan, Olive boarded in a large room under close supervision of the austere nuns who wore long, dark gray gowns with white habits. Across the courtyard was the chapel where they worshiped, perched at the edge of a plateau, looking out toward the mountains to the east.

Students were given English names after saints.[31] The virgin-martyr Santa Oliva di Palermo, Olive's namesake, was a Sicilian nobleman's daughter of steadfast faith who was banished to Tunisia, where she worked miracles until she was eventually tortured and beheaded at a young age.[32] Much like Olive, there is no official record of Santa Oliva, who is omitted in the church's Latin hagiology; and much like Olive, Santa Oliva was sanctified by popular tradition. Mother Superior could not possibly have predicted how apt a name they chose for Erjie.

Olive's older brothers, Edward and Jimmy, were given their English names at a boarding school modeled on Eton[33] that prepared sons of prominent ruling families to be leaders in the British tradition with Western values.

Olive did not take to the Catholic spiritual education at the convent. Early on, Mother Superior had instructed new students to seek out a best friend with whom they could share a spiritual bond with the Lord. It was a strange proposition for Olive, who didn't quite fit in with the other girls.

Olive was constantly getting in trouble for things like smoking, which most young girls didn't do. Olive was accustomed to wearing trousers and complained about the matronly blue overall dresses they were required to wear as uniforms.

When Olive had asked a pretty classmate to be her friend, she teased Olive. "No way," the classmate said, "you have short hair, like a boy!"

Olive automatically commanded respect from passersby at home in Kokang, but at school, alongside the other girls from noble families, she suffered the indignities of being bullied like an ordinary person.

Feeling fed up, she started to keep the pistol her father had given her in her backpack, to make sure when she was next teased in the courtyard by the bully classmate, she would be prepared.

"You have no reason to be disrespectful to me," Olive said, puffing up her chest, gesturing with her hands like a gun, when the day inevitably came, "I can defend myself if needed."

The bully classmate thought surely Olive was joking. "Oh yeah? Show me!"

Olive was never one to be accused of being a coward. And as she drew the gun from her backpack to dispel any doubts, screams arose from their corner of the courtyard, alarming the nuns.

Mother Superior was so scandalized, Olive was banned from the school. Olive didn't mind being expelled because it meant she could leave the convent and could go back home where she didn't have to worry about following so many rules, and people weren't so alarmed by guns. Olive was mystified by the commotion and the gossip it caused. After all, it wasn't like she had brandished the gun—and besides, where else was she supposed to carry it, if not in a backpack?[33]

Olive went to finish school in the cosmopolitan provincial capital of Kunming in China and stayed with Edward's new mother-in-law.

Figure 2.2.　Chinese soldiers advancing up the Burma Road ca. 1941.
US NATIONAL ARCHIVES.

She was a woman of leisure who took breakfast in bed at noon, then played mahjong and smoked opium with a collection of well-connected anti-communists before retiring late. They were loyalists to Generalissimo Chiang Kai-shek, who waged deadly anti-communist suppression campaigns.[35]

Shortly after arriving, Olive's school closed because another girls' school for the blind was hit by Japanese bombs that came pelting Kunming for days from above.[36] When the air-raid sirens sounded, Olive rushed outside to cheer the cartoonishly fierce-looking planes of the Flying Tigers buzz overhead. The newly formed special unit of American and Chinese mercenary pilots flew Warhawk planes, with noses painted to look like shark teeth.[37]

Along with their chief, the American General Claire Lee Chennault, they were lionized by the press for their heroic contributions to the allied effort in World War II. Olive was infatuated with their jeeps and jackets, and whenever she saw them in the streets, she called out to them in English, hoping to get a ride or chewing gum.[38]

By 1942, the Flying Tigers could no longer protect Burma from a Japanese invasion. The Japanese left devastation in their wake as they fanned out, killing, looting, and burning nearly anybody or anything they encountered before they arrived at Kokang's southern boundary that May. A column of invaders marched north beyond the last paved road, through the treacherous hills, then came and ransacked the family court as a warning before ensconcing themselves in a monastery.[39]

When the Japanese next came upon the family court, they found nobody but a loyal family servant guarding it. A childhood fever had left him deaf and unable to speak, so when they tortured him to extract intelligence, he could not understand them, nor could he produce information if he tried. He was doused in kerosene and burned to death, before the rest of the compound was set alight. His charred corpse was later found among the ashes.[40]

The family guard of thirty men would no longer be enough to defend Kokang from the thousands of Japanese troops advancing toward the Chinese border. Women and children of the family went into hiding. From a central headquarters along with his headmen, Olive's father declared a state of emergency, drafted an army of local recruits, and founded the Kokang Self-Defense Force, the army Olive would eventually lead. Fifteen hundred offended Kokang recruits, including nearly every single one of Olive's male relatives, joined the war effort.[41]

In Kunming, Olive's father came to appeal to Generalissimo Chiang for military assistance. Olive's father could not take her pleas to join the resistance seriously—he thought of her as too young and, of course, female. He hoped the worst of the war was over when he left Olive behind and returned to his central headquarters in Kokang as colonel and joint-commander of a division of Generalissimo Chiang's troops to aid in Kokang's resistance against the Japanese.[42] Olive was separated from the family but listened to daily radio broadcasts about Japanese planes downed by the Flying Tigers.

One morning in September 1943, Olive's entire family narrowly escaped a massacre in the safehouse where they had just been sleeping.

An opportunistic relative schemed with Chinese troops in their midst to revive an old bloodline's claim to power and initiated a mutiny. He intended to turn Kokang over to the Chinese after the war and had begun referring to himself as the new chieftain. The first casualty was Olive's third brother, who had trained as an officer, and was shot in his own garrison at the age of twenty-one. Olive's father broke his leg in the dramatic escape, and ended up in prison.[43]

Back in Kunming, US allies equipped Olive's Uncle Yang Wen Can with a team of spies to help restore the family's rule in Kokang. The Office of Strategic Services—the precursor to the CIA—created a first-of-its-kind guerilla detachment. The OSS 101 Detachment was to gather intelligence behind enemy lines, relying on cooperation with local tribal forces.[44]

Uncle Yang Wen Can returned to Kokang and personally commanded the execution of the mutineer by firing squad, mercilessly putting an end to all his relatives, sparing only his mother and sister. The 101 Detachment helped Uncle Yang Wen Can clear a drop zone for much-needed supplies General Chennault's Flying Tigers airlifted to them. Kokang remained one of the only parts of the country that did not fall to the Japanese during the war, but the internal bickering among the relatives made it impossible to launch any large-scale attacks.[45]

Elsewhere, however, 101 Detachment missions were wildly successful, largely due to the talents of none other than American Baptist missionaries from the Young family. By then, the Young family had tens of thousands of converts among the tribespeople in China's and Burma's borderlands, at their mission in a town south of Kunming in Yunnan.

Unable to return to China, Harold worked from Burma. His brother, recruited for his knowledge of numerous tribal languages, organized and recruited tribespeople in raids on Japanese soldiers, stationed near Kokang's front, who ambushed their human targets in the same finely attuned ways they hunted animal prey in the jungles. They proved critical to the final drive against the Japanese.

Some people tell stories about a young teenage Olive, fighting alongside heroic Uncle Yang Wen Can against the Japanese. In fact, as the tragedies unfolded, Olive was in Kunming, falling in love with a woman for the first time.[46]

CHAPTER THREE

Man, Woman, Myth, or Legend?

AFTER HEARING OLIVE'S FAMILY HAD OWNED A CHINESE RESTAURANT in Yangon, I started dining at every one I could find. One evening at a dumpling house with large red lamps in the windows, a friendly patron at a nearby table assured me the Yang family restaurant at which he had once dined was no more.

"Olive washed her hands in the golden basin," he said, using an idiomatic Chinese expression meaning she had retired and used her ill-gotten wealth toward washing her hands of the sins of her past. He explained Olive was now quietly enjoying her twilight years in a convent as a nun making merit before death somewhere around Yangon, after donating her wealth to the lord Buddha, so she could stay out of trouble.

"Nonsense," his wife chimed in. "Once, the Yangs owned all of Kokang, but Lo Hsing Han double-crossed them. Now it is all Lo Hsing Han's family in control of Kokang—even their old restaurant belongs to him. You'll have to go to Taiwan to find her," she said.

Just in case, I began to look up the nunneries nearby, even though the idea of Olive swaddled in pink robes hiding in plain sight had the air of a fairytale. It turned out Olive had a lookalike cousin who had been living as a nun in Yangon until her death, and the two were constantly confused for one another.

"She was such a hero. We all wanted to meet her because of the people she saved after the '88 Uprising," an Australian aid worker said to me one evening over drinks, referring to the uprising that had preceded Than Shwe's rise to power. "Olive's smugglers helped Americans escape the country."

I later realized this was an erroneous belief commonly held by people who thought the film *Beyond Rangoon* was based on a true story.

I eventually found a run-down private mahjong parlor owned by a prominent Kokang family where Olive had once played. The stony-faced proprietress told me in its heyday, all Yangon's Kokang-speakers came to gamble in that room. In fact, she had lived around the corner, and her political party, from which she was promptly ousted, had been founded there.

I was shocked to hear Olive had been a politician.

"Why would you want to be looking for her, anyway? I would be careful if I was you," she warned me, curtly. "Those Yangs never get along, forcing other people to pick sides in their sibling rivalry, using other people to get rich. You'll have trouble getting anybody to talk about her here. Around here, we are all Lo Hsing Han's people."

I was repeatedly reminded that Lo was Olive's rival. The reversal in the two Kokang families' fortunes was allegedly a direct result of Lo's decision to betray the Yang family and cut a deal with the government. Indeed, Lo's vast opium empire which produced the vast wealth he laundered through his conglomerate had been built in what was once the Yang's territory.

"Do you know any of her former soldiers who would know some of her battle stories?" I asked.

"Battle stories? She never fought in any battles herself. She just sent her boys to fight for her."

I couldn't reconcile the statement with the stories I'd heard of Olive's reputation for being a quick draw with a sharp shot who rode like she was being chased by the devil. The son of a decorated general of the defunct Communist Party of Burma had assured me she was a battle hero of great courage, who had taught all the greatest Kokang warriors how to be soldiers.

One evening, at a downtown speakeasy, I spotted the main source of English-language stories about Olive: Bertil Lintner had been a Burma expert since before I could talk. He was blacklisted by the government for over a decade and had only recently been allowed to travel in the country again.

He authored vignettes across a smattering of books claiming she had led one thousand troops by the age of twenty-four and that with the help of the CIA and her army "Olive's Boys," became an essential pioneer of the modern opium trade in the Golden Triangle. Bertil also identified Olive as bisexual and by the moniker Miss Hairy Legs. All of which were details I could not yet independently verify. It soon seemed Bertil couldn't, either.

"Well, she did have a son, so we know she was bisexual." Bertil said, with a lip full of Swedish chewing tobacco, admitting he had never met Olive.

Giving birth seemed like iron-clad evidence of a heterosexual encounter, I agreed. But Bertil had a more old-fashioned view of sexuality and was very authoritative about nearly everything. He insisted his sources had sworn him to secrecy—which made it difficult to check his facts. When I asked him whether Miss Hairy Legs was a cryptonym, he said he could not tell me. But it was unlike Bertil not to know, and he was infamously tight-lipped about how he got his information.

The bartender had started closing up early, because the ward official had imposed a curfew, which Bertil took as a welcome cue to gather his things. Panicked, I finally asked him more directly how he knew about Olive's involvement with the CIA.

"We have reason to believe she was a CIA asset for the Secret Army," Bertil said, referring to the group of stubborn Chinese remnants in the Burmese borderlands who refused to surrender to the communists in the 1950s. Because the CIA could not admit to supporting them, they were eventually known as the Secret Army, long before they formed the intelligence and logistics basis for the wars in Laos and Vietnam.

"I can't do your work for you. It's in the historical record," Bertil said before heading out the door.

No lead about Olive Yang seemed too absurd to follow, which produced ever more rabbit holes to investigate and the sneaking suspicion that she simply could not be found. Every night I went to bed believing that she must be dead and then woke up thinking that just one more phone call wouldn't hurt.

But after a few months of searching, I stood stunned in my apartment holding my phone, elated that I had just found Olive, shouting with maniacal joy. "She's alive!"

A parliamentarian in Shan State I had called knew where the legendary character was living in his constituency. He referred to Olive as a Kokang national hero and saw himself as doing the same work she had once done: getting citizenship documents for people of Chinese descent.[1]

"Olive is the champion of our people's rights," he explained.

Olive had been ailing for a few years now and was living in Muse, where her stepson was taking care of her.

"He's sort of a big deal, the stepson. He's, you know, a big important guy. He has a trading company for cows," the parliamentarian said.

Apparently, anybody who wanted to talk to her had to talk to him first, and he went by simply "Master Duan."

I greeted Master Duan on the phone and introduced myself as an American journalist who wanted to speak to his mother. It didn't strike me as odd until the words came out of my mouth.

He appeared to hold the receiver for Olive, who spoke a greeting in Chinese.

After months of searching, I finally heard Olive's voice on the phone in the form of a monosyllabic greeting.

"She can't speak so clearly these days on the phone because of her teeth," Duan explained apologetically in heavily accented Chinese. He said he would welcome a visit the following week and it was better to talk to her in person.

"Call me when you're in Muse," he said referring to the remote, bustling trade hub straddling the Chinese border in northeastern Shan State where he lived, before abruptly hanging up.

So one week later, I was on the road to Muse together with a translator who had taken the English name "Democracy Rain." He was a religious Christian who wore torn jeans and seemed excited by the idea of meeting such a legendary rebel as I briefed him on the plan.

The road grew steeper and more winding, narrowing to a single lane as it crept up the mountains, until we arrived thoroughly nauseated outside of the dusty sprawling town that spilled all the way across the border. The part of Muse on the Chinese side of the border had a cluster of high-rises and casinos that contrasted starkly with the more dilapidated buildings on the Myanmar side.

Travel to Muse was generally inadvisable because it was so rife with conflict and armed groups; several journalists had recently been either injured or inexplicably detained or deported while working there. So when the immigration official at the local police station asked how long we would stay and what we were doing, he also warned us not to get into any trouble.

I called Duan as instructed, who promised to meet us at our hotel, despite seeming exasperated on the phone. Not long after checking in and unpacking, I received a call from the front desk claiming the police arrived in the hotel lobby asking for me.

When I went to the lobby, I was surprised to find two Chinese men dressed as civilians in regular polo shirts, who appeared nonthreateningly paunchy and diminutive. They asked me who I was and for a letter of introduction and my passport information. Then they said they would like to search my room.

It was an extremely unusual request. I had been followed by spies on motorbikes on previous reporting trips, and I had been asked to identify myself by immigration police, but I had never before been confronted by plainclothes officers like that and I wasn't sure how to respond. The receptionist seemed skeptical of the visitors and gently shook his head.

My phone vibrated. I glanced down to see a series of text messages from Democracy Rain.

"it's a trap!!! they're not real police!!!"

I had gathered as much but wondered what sort of trap Democracy Rain meant exactly and how he knew that, given that he was inconveniently absent. I made a pearl-clutching gesture and exclaimed loudly that it would be inappropriate for men to search the room of a single woman traveling, hoping the receptionist would offer to supervise.

The pretend police exchanged tense glances with one another. They relented on their demand to search my room but then offered to wait while I wrote my letter of introduction. As I handed them the letter, I asked the two men who they worked for. They refused to answer.

"Is it Duan?"

They nodded.

"Ah, so you work for his company. The cow company?"

The two exchanged looks again.

"No," one of them finally exclaimed, "it's not a cow company!"

They promptly left with the paperwork and began to speak to one another in hushed tones. I watched them leave through the glass doors of the hotel and walk down the street to their car. The minute they had turned a corner, Democracy Rain popped up from behind the wall of the kiosk next door and walked into the hotel, a stricken look on his face.

"What did they say to you?" he asked.

"They wanted to search my room . . ." I was unable to finish my sentence.

"They're not police, I heard them. It's a trap!" Democracy Rain repeated.

"Don't worry, I didn't let them," I told Democracy Rain, who seemed relieved that I had made the right decision. "What exactly do you mean when you say trap?"

"Maybe a bomb or something, or they want to plant something in your room," Democracy Rain suggested, still shaken from the encounter with the men.

It was extremely perplexing that they wanted to search my room but planting bombs seemed so outlandish that the possibility hadn't occurred to me. I didn't want to upset Democracy Rain by getting unsettled, but that, too, appeared to upset him.

Later that evening I called Duan and invited him for a beer. He refused. I asked if he had seen my passport information and the letter of introduction and if that would help explain what I was here for at all. He said he had and refused to see me, with or without Olive. I hoped Duan might change his mind about seeing me if I just remained patient, but I knew I was pushing my luck.

As far as I was concerned, Olive was being sequestered by some-one who would never allow me to meet her—but why? Why did his underlings refuse to say who their employer was exactly? What exactly did he have to be so paranoid about?

"Did you tell him you were a journalist who worked for Voice of America?" Democracy Rain asked.

I nodded.

"He probably thinks you work for the CIA, then."

I had just about had it with people falsely accusing me of being a spy when I told them I worked for Voice of America. I knew I wasn't a spy, but Democracy Rain made a good point. I seemed to be the last person in the office to figure out that the CIA had previously violated its own policy of not using reporters as covers for their spies. Decades ago, officers already fully employed by the CIA had permission to collect double compensation when Voice of America hired them for part-time work as a cover.[2]

It was hard to imagine how I would win the trust of a man who was under the impression my intention was to gather intelligence for the US government.

"I don't think his company is a cow company," Democracy Rain said, as he became increasingly nervous and suspicious. "Why else would they want to search you, unless they think you are armed?"

"One of the men said as much," I agreed. A man with a live-stock export business so powerful that he had men at his disposal to search a hotel room on short notice in the Golden Triangle was likely exporting more than just cows. I worried we may have unwittingly poked a hornet's nest, and that the longer we stayed, the more chances there were for something—who knew what, exactly—to go wrong.

Back in the safety of Yangon, roughly one month after the failed visit, my luck finally changed when I met someone who knew Olive well but wasn't too afraid to talk to me.

"She was my favorite," Lynn said, bubbling over with adoration when we spoke on the phone. Olive had always taken a special liking to the girls in the family, especially her favorite little grand-niece, Lynn. Now in her twenties, Lynn was a celebrity in certain circles after making gossip-rag headlines a few years prior on a televised modeling competition filmed in Singapore. Her fascinating heritage was completely elided on the show.

In fact, not even her best friends knew much about her family: it was too complicated to explain to most people and invited judgment because of the family's involvement in the drug trade.

"It's not a secret—we just don't tell anybody. It's easier that way," Lynn explained. The result was that often even very good friends of hers had no idea where exactly she came from.

On a hot and cloudy afternoon, I visited the house where she'd grown up which was surrounded by a high wall with a spiked gate. Lynn's mother, Wu Tse, met me under the portico. She was in her late fifties and wore her graying hair in a short, stylish bowl cut, and bore an uncanny resemblance to Olive when she smiled.

She took me through the backyard to the bungalow where Olive had lived for some time in the nineties, near the water's edge of the northern shore of the lake. Sometimes, Lynn would spend time on the porch of the bungalow near the water, playing make-believe bandits, and Olive would advise her on what sorts of weapons to carry. Sometimes, Olive would play tricks with her false teeth, furtively taking them out to hide them around the living room, leaving others to be frightened when they found them at an unexpected moment. Olive and Lynn shared a quality of mischief, and her parents joked if they spent too much time together she'd turn into a soldier.

"The children used to play outside with Olive here, oh, nearly twenty years ago now, because they were afraid of seeing her feet," Wu Tse said, and then explained that Olive's feet had been bound when she was little, and her feet were frighteningly mangled. I couldn't imagine someone with bound feet capable of doing the amount of riding she was alleged to have done: it hadn't occurred to me as a possibility.

"How did Olive ride with bound feet?" I asked, gobsmacked by the revelation.

"Olive did everything with bound feet. The children would wait for her to put on shoes and come outside because they thought her feet were so scary looking," Wu Tse said.

Figure 3.1.   Left to right: Olive's fourth sister Jane, Olive Yang, Edward's wife Lu Shwin Zhen, pictured in the 1990s.
YANG FAMILY PRIVATE COLLECTION.

On one occasion, when Lynn was not yet an adolescent, a man with an entourage dropped by the house. When Lynn later inquired who the visitor was, her mother tried to downplay what an important visitor they had just received. "Sweetheart, that was Lo Hsing Han," she explained in a shushed voice, indicating to Lynn she shouldn't advertise the detail widely. "He used to be the security guard for your grandfather and for Uncle Olive."

"I didn't know how unusual it was to receive visits from people like that until I was older," Lynn told me, swearing Lo had left a bag of money with Olive before departing.

Because so many other people seemed to think so, Lynn had always known that Olive was special or important—as was her grandfather and any other number of her relatives— but didn't quite know exactly why. As she grew older, some stories she heard about Olive made sense, some didn't. Some that seemed true, some that didn't. "I don't even know what's real some of the time, there are some questions about Olive I've never gotten answers to, so I don't even know if I believe the stories that she worked for the CIA," Lynn said.

She sighed deeply. "But I have fond memories of my Uncle Olive."

Uncle? I had never considered the possibility that Olive might have been an uncle and not just manly with hairy legs, as described by Bertil. Lynn had been using female pronouns with male honorifics. It wasn't uncommon for Burmese or Chinese speakers to confuse pronouns when speaking English, but everybody I had spoken to had referred to Olive as a woman.

"Do people say 'he' or 'she'?" I asked.

"Both, really," Lynn said. While all the other female relatives went by "aunty," Olive had preferred to use the title "uncle," like other male relatives and had used male pronouns in Burmese because she felt it was more respectful. "I guess you could say she was trans, but we didn't really talk about it when she was living with us. Everybody just accepted it, and let Uncle Olive be."

"But also, back then it wasn't so common to be gay, and it was embarrassing for everybody in the family. Now of course, things are different, but back then nobody wanted to talk about it," Wu Tse said.

"Is that why they called her 'Miss Hairy Legs'?" I asked.

"What? Who is they?" Wu Tse was insulted and insisted nobody in the family had ever called Olive that, and she had never been that hairy.

"Bertil wrote in his books that that's what they called her," I said, pointing down to my own legs.

"Why would they say that? People always think they can make up such nonsense about our family, especially about Olive because Olive is gay," Wu Tse said touching her forehead, as though even thinking about it was tedious and insulting. "We don't even have a way to say that name in the Kokang language."

"Do you think he was wrong about Olive and the CIA, too?"

"The CIA? You never know with Olive . . ." Wu Tse said and raised an eyebrow, sensing I might ask more questions. "There are many stories to tell about Olive, she told stories all the time, but I can't really remember any of it now. I'm sorry I won't be very useful to you because I don't know very much."

Whenever Wu Tse was about to say something interesting, she seemed not to be able to remember.

"They always accuse us of trafficking drugs or working with the CIA, but I never knew anything about it. All these foreigners come and write nonsense like Olive has hairy legs because she is gay, or they assume we are all opium smokers because we are Chinese. Not even Olive was an opium smoker."

I took this as a clear warning not to write nonsense about the family. Wu Tse had cast just enough doubt on the accuracy of the elusive character portrayed in books for me to question every detail I'd heard.

Perhaps Olive had been the bisexual CIA asset Miss Hairy Legs who was a commander in the CIA's failed invasion of China; perhaps not. Because Olive could never speak about her life publicly, her story had been told through others, leaving the world with a confusing catalog of conflicting, unconfirmed half-truths that sounded apocryphal.

At first, I had been looking for what I thought was a woman in a grave; then, a bisexual warlady in men's fatigues with hairy legs. Now, I was looking for a more mysterious, perhaps misunderstood, uncle with bound feet.

CHAPTER FOUR

Olive's Coming-Out

BY THE TIME OLIVE DEVELOPED INTO A BEAUTIFUL AND OTHERWISE DESIRABLE marriage prospect, people said she already had a widespread reputation for violent outbursts directed at male suitors.

Some told the story of a prince who came to vie for Olive's hand in marriage. He narrowly evaded death when his entourage approached the Yang family court for an engagement ceremony. A single gunshot flew past his horse, injuring his attendant. They returned without ever stepping through the Yang family's gate.

Then, a beautiful bandit was seen riding a white steed across Burma's hillocks. They said she was a wealthy landowner's daughter who had escaped during the Japanese invasion, learned guerilla warfare tactics from a British officer who broke her heart—and captured the hearts of many as she put her newfound military prowess to use.

Villagers assumed it was Olive, jilted and full of vengeance on her white horse. She charged at Burmese sentries on the moonlit riverbank of the Salween, where the Burmese commanders swore she'd been killed. But even after everybody said she had died, she was seen again ransacking more villages. The outsmarted Burma Army commanders had to admit she had used a very good strategy, by allowing them to believe she was vanquished.

Shortly after her wedding, other Shan princesses were convinced Olive had killed her husband. When a short-haired Olive showed up at caravan trading posts without a husband as chaperone, any man who found her beautiful soon learned the rumor that she was a vicious murderous widow.

One follower could attest: after one too many of her husband's repeated advances in their marriage bed, Olive reached for the weapon she kept conveniently beneath her pillow, and a gunfight ensued. Outmatched by Olive's pair of pistols, her husband was never to be seen or heard from again.[1] Among her gaggle of horseback followers—bandits, criminals in exile or escaped prisoners, each with a checkered past that drove them to resort to banditry to make a living—Olive's story was not unusual.

Many years later Olive's husband was very much alive and incarcerated on cellblock number two of Insein Prison. He had to deny stories of the insulting notion that Olive was a man-slayer on the loose after shooting her husband dead.

Olive had shot at him, that much was true. But he insisted it was only after a string of refusals led him to suggest marrying a second concubine. Only then, Olive became violent, and fired her pistol at him in a fit of jealous rage.

"I was a good match for her! You know, a stolen wife[2] is a good wife," Olive's husband reminded a fellow inmate, suggesting the legendary Olive Yang had desired him when they were initially betrothed. "But once we got married, she suddenly went cold on me. And humiliated me by refusing to appear whenever I summoned her."

He explained that she had worn the two guns at her hips, even when they were in their court, and she would point to them every time he broached the subject of their marital relations.

"She was just too overbearing. I like to think that a good man doesn't fight a woman," he insisted.[3]

Olive fell in love with a woman several years before being forced into marriage and motherhood, sometime in 1944, amid near-daily air-raid sirens in Kunming.

Warlords threatened insurrection; there were troops and spies everywhere and looters among them. One day, not long before the allies declared victory, Olive accompanied her mother to the bank where they had deposited the Yang family treasure, a chest filled with all the state funds in gold and silver for safekeeping during the war. Because the account was so valuable, they were assigned their own teller to attend them.[4]

Jean was a sophisticated, fair-skinned young beauty with dark red curls, who spoke English with a broad, lilting Scottish accent she inherited from her mother. Jean dressed elegantly and attracted the attention of many young soldiers stationed in Kunming.

Olive's mother knew immediately she had fallen in love with Jean, because whenever she went to the bank Olive wanted to come along. Jean was incredibly independent for a young unmarried woman and did not adhere to the traditional gender roles Olive was inured to seeing. Her parents had been missionaries—she was born in China and spoke fluent Chinese—but she had chosen a life for herself away from the church, finished school, and was making a living on her own.

At age eighteen, Olive was getting old for an unmarried girl, gallivanting around town getting into trouble. Olive had repeatedly said she was not interested in marrying a man, a preposterous idea for Olive's parents, who saw their daughters as temporary relatives to be married off to other ruling families.[5] An unmarried woman had no man to whom she could attach her station and would live in isolation and poverty.

Olive's second brother, Jimmy, was dispatched to take Olive home. Before they departed, they visited the bank one final time to wrap up their affairs. Jimmy finally understood why Olive was so reluctant to leave: much like his sister, he fell in love with Jean at first sight. Jimmy made an alluring bachelor as a handsome, young military officer with a large bank account. He had taken up the anti-communist struggle working at Generalissimo Chiang's military intelligence department.

Olive pleaded with Jean to come visit them in Kokang when she bid her farewell, and Jean agreed to come in a few months' time.

The Kokang to which Olive returned was left desolate by the war. Hundreds of civilians had died, among them relatives, neighbors, and friends. The family court sat charred atop its hill, and their humble mud thatch hospital was destroyed. The cobblestone lane surrounding the temple in Old Street Village where the market once stood badly needed repairs.[6]

Yet what proved most challenging was convincing their father to allow Edward to build a school. Most people in Kokang could not read, including some of the headmen. Their father believed it would spell chaos to allow the people to learn to read and write, especially the women, who were nearly all illiterate. But Edward managed to hire a few teachers from China and limited students in the first class to the sons of their headmen.[7] The headmen believed allowing womenfolk to read was bad luck, so at first no women were taught to read.

For two generations, Yang daughters had intermarried with the Duan family, the rulers of a nearby township just across the Salween River on who were vassals to Sao Hom Hpa. So just like her aunt and her aunt before her, Olive was promised to the nearby chieftain's son, Duan Chaowen.

The Duan family came with gifts to set a date for the traditional engagement ceremony, known as "kill the chicken," during which they would sacrifice a bird and feast. By the time they were promised to one another, Duan was already a war veteran in his twenties, who had fought alongside American and British soldiers against the Japanese. Even so, by all accounts, Duan was terrified of hot-tempered Olive, who was already known to be prone to violent outbursts, before he even met her. At their first face-to-face meeting, Olive found her future husband tall and handsome but infuriatingly slow, speaking with an opium smoker's sluggish affect.[8]

The chicken was decapitated, then its eyes were pulled out through its beak, so the geomancer could read their hexagrams. They set an auspicious date for the wedding ceremony several months out. Once the chicken was killed, the marriage contract legally bound Duan to produce an heir: an upsetting prospect for Olive, who abhorred the thought of sex with a man and dreaded pregnancy. But the families proceeded, and in a sense, Olive had no choice.

In the year that led up to Olive's wedding, Burma gained independence from Britain, and Kokang became an independent state. Almost exactly fifty years after their one-eyed great-granduncle's unfavorable deal, a

Yang family delegation asserted their ancestor's unfulfilled wish for internal autonomy at a meeting before a council of Shan chieftains. Their odious overlord Sao Hom Hpa begrudgingly agreed to release them.[9]

So, at the military civilian rally to mark the momentous occasion of Burma's independence on January 4, 1948, Edward raised the new Burmese flag as the heir of an independent Kokang State, and their father's title was elevated to *sawbwa*, one of the thirty-three "Lords of the Sky."[10]

Though they now held the same title as *sawbwa* Sao Hom Hpa, he was made Special Commissioner of Shan State in Lashio, so they would have to answer to him anyway. And most upsettingly, a clause in the constitution required all hereditary rulers to relinquish their noble titles and retire. The date of impending doom was set for ten years out.

When Jean finally came to visit, she found Kokang was perhaps more rugged than expected. Jimmy had personally accompanied Jean from Kunming to make sure she wasn't attacked in the wild jungles along the way. Just as they were approaching the border crossing on the final stretch of their journey, a Chinese communist official suddenly took them into custody. They were locked in a filthy pigsty for several hours before a relative came to rescue them.[11]

During Jean's stay, her mother sent word she would have to cut her visit in Kokang short and make plans to leave for home back in Scotland immediately. Mao Zedong had declared China for the communists, the entirety of the border was sent into upheaval, and there had been an uprising in Kunming. It was too dangerous for them to stay.

Jimmy, unwilling to let Jean leave so easily, confessed he had fallen in love. He proposed they marry and begged her to stay. It was a complex proposal for Jean, for reasons that were unknown to most of the family: Jean had a secret baby daughter from a previous marriage, who was being raised by her mother as her own. The little girl's father had been one of Chennault's men, a Flying Tigers pilot who had disappeared from Jean's life. To marry Jimmy would mean leaving her own daughter behind.

Jimmy was convincing, if not coercive. He didn't seem too keen on helping her leave, and after the frightening incident in the pigsty, Jean wasn't sure if she knew how to get back on her own. The way their son

Map 4.1. Map of Kokang and North Hsenwi after World War II.

later told the story, Jean was essentially kidnapped and had no choice but to make the best of it. Jean eventually grew to love Jimmy and never spoke of her first daughter after that. Neither did Jimmy.

According to the siblings, when Jean and Jimmy announced they were engaged soon thereafter, Olive's foul mood was hard to ignore. Jean knew the choice to marry Jimmy would feel like a betrayal to Olive. Olive refused to speak to either of them for some time. To the family, this was a coming-out. Olive didn't need to say it, but because she made no secret of her feelings for Jean, this was how most people in the family learned that Olive preferred women.

They had known previously that Olive was boyish and seemed to prefer spending time with girls, but they had not considered the possibility that Olive might be romantically interested in women, much less that Olive might not quite be a woman exactly.

Olive took her moods out on her mother and argued bitterly about having to marry Duan. According to Kokang custom, had Olive decided to break the marriage contract, the family would have to repay the groom's dowry gifts ninefold. Finally her mother offered to bribe her. "How many guns will it take?" she asked.

"How many guns can you get?" Olive replied. As a wedding gift from her mother, she was given two pistols and a leather holster.

The Duan's ancestors were Chinese merchants who escaped to Burma and said the first ruler in their dynasty had been given land by the great Burmese King Bayinnaung during an elephant-mounted advance and sacking of Siam.[12] Ever since the Kachins had escaped Olive's grandfather's wrath, Duan's native village was one of the few Chinese ones among the Kachins on Sao Hom Hpa's land.

Traditionally, when ordinary Kachin men wanted to marry a young girl, they first plotted to steal a lock of her hair to be tested by a sorcerer or geomancer. If the match was deemed propitious, the man would arrange with his friends to kidnap the object of his desire, sometimes without the parents' knowledge. The wealthier the man, the more wives he could abduct.* Sao Hom Hpa, who tithed many lands with great riches of jade and gold, could afford seven wives.

Olive's wedding ceremony to a nobleman's son was a staged abduction, however, accompanied by a small armed entourage for the days-long ride west of the Salween to Duan's ancestral land. Just as all her sisters and brothers' wives had, Olive wore a traditional silk red sheath dress when she kowtowed together with her husband for the first time as a married couple.

The tension in the household was immediate following Olive's arrival, due to the one obligation of married life neither the terrified Duan nor the infuriated Olive could evade. They were required by law to produce an heir. In fact, if five years elapsed without a pregnancy, the

---

* Alan Winnington, *Slaves of the Cool Mountains*, Serif, London, 1959, pp. 45, 178.

marriage could be annulled. Olive took this legal loophole as a challenge, and her mother's wedding gift soon came in handy.

It was the traditional duty of a woman to resist her husband's advances for as long as possible—first with pretenses and excuses, and finally with biting and scratching. An acquiescent wife would be regarded as being of questionable nobility. Whenever Duan proposed they go to bed together, Olive began to distract him by picking fights. Duan had an unabashed and unrestrained affection for his opium pipe; his habit was to withdraw to their bed and smoke until sleep came. So Olive scolded him about the smell to escape his more insistent moments.

"You stink!" she told him one time, "and your opium pipe has made the bedroom smelly."

Duan later told prison inmates Olive had devised elaborate plots to prevent him from being able to relax in his own bed. On one occasion, she had called one of Duan's family guards to come with his rifle and stand at a new post in the courtyard outside their bedroom window. She instructed him to set up such that he could easily target their bed. "If you see your master smoking in bed, I give you permission to shoot. In fact, I command you to shoot him."

Figure 4.1. Olive (believed to have been photographed shortly after her wedding) with long hair at the temple in Lashio. YANG FAMILY COLLECTION.

Then she added for good measure, "and if you don't shoot him, I'll shoot you."

The guard trained his weapon directly on Duan's pillow.

For several days, Duan left Olive alone, and the air in their bed chambers was fragrant and clear. But Duan eventually gave in to a craving on a subsequent night and crawled under their bed with his pipe, conveniently out of view of the bedroom window.

As the scent filled the home, an alarmed family guard rushed into the bedroom, only to find Olive already in the room, pistol drawn, and Duan cowering under the bed, begging for his life.

Almost as soon as Olive came to live with Duan, robbers came to the government bank in Lashio holding Sao Hom Hpa's state funds, kidnapping police officers and soldiers. Because Duan's family paid tithes to Sao Hom Hpa, he was summoned with his men to help restore the peace. The well-planned attack left stunned guards bleary eyed, as the group made away with their loot. But one soldier swore once the smoke had cleared, he saw a beautiful maiden on a pure white stallion, flying through the night, who seemed to be directing them.[13] The fearless beauty Ma Khin Nyunt appeared to be roaming the border and struck fear into the hearts of men as an assassin for hire, cooperating with communist bandits.[14]

Duan fought valiantly when more robbers came to clean out whatever was left in the bank, this time Kachin insurgents with leftover World War II rifles and smoke bombs. After a foiled plot to kidnap Sao Hom Hpa, the maiden on the white steed was seen again, looting cattle.

Remote villages in Kokang were attacked by petty criminals who robbed their chickens and rice in waves. So Edward and Jimmy began recruiting volunteers into a force at their newly established military academy. Before the first training period had even concluded, they confronted a gang of rapscallions in a village where a headman had been murdered.[15]

To avenge the deaths of three officials killed in the recent violence, Olive's father summoned a local mercenary who went by the name Fat Huang to kill an exiled relative whom they suspected was behind the violence.

Fat Huang was a round-waisted, thick-lipped ruffian who haunted the mountain routes southward of Kokang. His specialty was armed robbery, for which he carried a pair of copper maces as weapons to threaten unsuspecting stranger merchants, traveling from afar.[16]

Some said to collect the bounty, Fat Huang had to prove he had been successful with an identifiable decapitated head. He was handsomely rewarded with silver for his service and used his reward to build a hideout on a hill surrounded by opium fields, where other bandits began to follow him and started robbing the roads. Behind his house was a cave filled with fire ants and pythons and had a chasm that was so deep, you couldn't hear when things hit the bottom.

Fat Huang and his bandits were said to have dropped in the heads of their victims, and soon the villagers began to call it the "falling hole." They believed those who passed the cave loudly would be visited by death within the month after offending the cave's spirits but could be appeased with offerings of liquor.

When Duan returned between deployments, his mother was eager to see her son fulfill his carnal duties as a husband. It caused her anxiety that her niece, Olive, would not submit to Duan. Their first few encounters were unsuccessful because Olive had resisted violently, reaching for her guns before Duan could approach her. Olive had made it clear sexual encounters with Duan were unwanted and was running out of excuses to tell the servants whenever he requested her presence in their bedchambers.

It is unclear exactly when, but while Duan was in the family court between deployments, his mother planned for him to lay with and impregnate Olive. Duan had survived battle only to have to risk his life in service to his ancestors; so his mother cleared the bedroom of weapons and prepared the bed. Olive's aunt had guards check Olive for guns.

She locked her niece and son in their room together. Duan and Olive were told they were not to leave until they had completed the task. Duan knew Olive would not go down without a fight. He was under so much pressure from his mother to finally consummate the marriage, he persisted through a legendary beating to get the job done.

Without guns at the ready, Olive had nothing available to her but her fists. Crashes and shouts came from their bedroom. Everybody in their court knew it was happening because the commotion it caused was so loud, but this time, no guardsmen rushed in to break up the fight. She began to throw objects, including the latrine pot.

Duan's approach was so forceful, no furious insults or physical struggle from Olive could stop him. Once they had finished, when the guardsmen finally opened the bedroom door, they found Duan battered, partially clothed, and soaked in urine.[17]

Olive was inconsolable: A pregnancy would tie her inextricably to her husband, with no available escape through an annulment. Even though Olive had been so violently defensive, on subsequent nights, Duan persisted with his requests for her presence in their bed chambers.

Then, Olive's father died. All the siblings and cousins returned to mourn him and to pay respects to the new *sawbwa*, Edward. When he buried his father, Edward made the extraordinary vow never to order the cruel punishments of execution or ending all relatives, under his rule.

"You're asking for trouble," said Uncle Yang Wen Can, who had just put down the mutiny.

Even though Edward was determined to keep his vow, the family's sense of indebtedness to the mercenary Fat Huang for assassinating a rival cousin was never forgotten. So long as he abided by the precept of "rabbits do not eat the grass beside their nests," meaning he terrorized only outsiders, he was allowed to continue his banditry without consequence. That is how Fat Huang became untouchable.[18]

During the weekslong funeral, a tribal feud raged in the wild borderlands near Savage Mountain, partially due to events following World War II nobody in Harold's family liked to talk about. First there was trouble with their Wa adherents. A Chinese communist official accused of extorting a churchgoer was hacked to death by Christian villagers. When word spread, rival tribes retaliated against them, burning their homes. Missionaries were accused of instigating unrest. As the burned villages were being rebuilt, communist officials came with a letter asking them to accept peaceful liberation. They had no choice; their church was shut down, and one of their pastors was jailed as the feuds escalated.[19]

Harold had briefly taken a job as superintendent of the Wa states to the British government, at the gateway of Savage Mountain on Kokang's southern border. He executed several powerful Wa warriors he deemed criminals for acts of treason helping the Japanese in World War II and angered one of the chieftains by collecting mineral samples near their mines. Harold's wife was furious to discover he had been living like a little emperor with several servants and concubines. The allure of tribal women who were uninhibited by Baptist sexual taboos proved too great for Harold to resist. Harold was asked to leave Burma and forced to retire as a missionary, too.

Harold's wife forgave him and chose to never speak of his mid-life crisis again, but Harold wanted to return to help his Wa adherents who were being persecuted, so he applied for a job with the CIA.

The very last county in Yunnan to be liberated by the Chinese Communist Party was the one that shared a border with Kokang. It was the ancestral home of a fearsome Wa warrior whose family had ruled for nearly six hundred years. A rival Wa tribe who had already accepted communist liberation helped drive him out. Hundreds fled the war cries, escaping across the border to Kokang to safety. Communists pursued them right across the border into Kokang, where there were skirmishes in Old Street Village.

Refugees flowed into the family court, including purged officials, like the young Chinese General Li Wen Huan and his bandit-suppression brigade, who were loyal to Generalissimo Chiang.

"Kokang is next. The communists want to take Kokang for China," General Li told Edward. The small communist battalion he had just fought were still at large in Kokang.

General Li and the Wa warriors swore they were determined to reconquer the ancestral land he had just fled.[20]

Edward decided to be merciful and allow them to stay, but possession of unlicensed guns was punishable by death, so Edward told them to keep their arms in a registry and made them promise not to cause any trouble. He designated Uncle Yang Wen Can's old central radio command garrison from World War II, which villagers called the 101 garrison.

Some said as soon as their father died, nobody could tell Olive what to do anymore. So she never went back to Duan's village. It was very rare for a woman to leave an unwanted marriage, and they often ended up devastated financially, or became house slaves.

Others said when Olive returned to Duan's village, she was in a panic as soon as she realized she was with child. She had been lucky that Duan hadn't been around to see her changing body. Olive would have to act fast and plan her escape before her belly started to show, so she could get her marriage annulled. She left Duan by the cover of night with the help of the merciless Fat Huang, in order to carry the child to term in secret in their hideaway.

Some said, as soon as she heard of a group of thugs from across the border carrying a flag in a Kokang village that read "Upper Burma Communist Government,"[21] nothing could stop her from heeding Generalissimo Chiang's call to resist the communists. And by the time anybody in Duan's court noticed, she was halfway to Kokang having already declared herself divorced and joined hands with General Li at the 101 garrison.

CHAPTER FIVE

A Curse on the House of Yang

WU TSE

A WIDELY HELD BELIEF AMONG YOUNGER GENERATIONS OF THE YANG family is that when Edward died in Lashio in 1971, the fulfillment of the family's curse was sealed.

For his daughter, Wu Tse, the exact moment of his passing was memorable: Shortly after he drew his last breath, there were thunder claps as storm clouds blew in, the skies parted, and an unseasonable rain pounded down on the roof, like an evil omen.

All Edward's children were gathered at his deathbed. Subjects came from around the state to pay their respects, and Olive's absence was noted.* Wu Tse recounted how, as his last moments neared, Edward had been plagued by just one regret: He had failed to transition the state of Kokang to a stable democratic rule in his lifetime.

When lightning struck as Edward lay in wake, Wu Tse was just a young teenager in a family that had run afoul of the government in a declining socialist dictatorship. They had little means to support themselves, and that storm marked not only the end of their fortunate lives, but also the beginning of decades of upheaval during which democratic rule eluded the entire country—and their ancestral homeland fell to communism.

---

* Hsu Wen Long, the deputy to Lo Hsing Han who betrayed Edward, famously came to apologize at his deathbed; Olive was confined to Rangoon at the time.

"They say the Yang men are cursed," Wu Tse had told me when recalling the day her father, Edward, died. "They say that's why there are no more Yangs to pass on the family name. I don't really believe in curses, but it is what they say, and I guess it's true," she said.

Whether real or imagined, for Edward and Olive's generation, the curse had served as a forbidding admonition doled out during scoldings from their mother.

Once, not long before Edward became chieftain, his mother was scolding him for gambling and smoking opium, behavior she felt was unbefitting of an heir. In anger, she shamed him with the prophecy that his generation was to be the last Yang generation of rulers.

"The demise of the Yang dynasty will commence after the eighth generation," Edward's mother reminded him. "Maybe you will be the one to cause it."

Perhaps it was these words that haunted Edward as he voiced his final regrets before his death.

Though their ancestor's geomancer's revelations had been vague, it was hard to argue a demise had not befallen the Yang Dynasty, timed just as predicted, after Edward's generation.

While Edward and his brothers had been fruitful, his own sons were unmarried or gay, so there were no grandsons born to bear the names prescribed by the Yang family generational poem. But, cursed after the eighth generation, the family name had ceased like the half-finished poem authored by their ancestor, before it could fulfill its promise of nobility and prosperity.[†]

The truncated first half of the Yang family's generational poem, roughly translated, prophetically proclaims that a cultural awakening will shake up the family.

The Yang family no longer ruled in any way or any place. The family seal and the family name, which had once commanded respect, no longer

---

† Taken in its entirety, the twenty-character poem spells a marvelous fate of wealth and glory for the Yang family as guardians of the frontier for twenty generations. 高才維有國，春文振家邦；世守本承继，富贵荣华昌。

carried administrative power anywhere. Kokang itself, the place where their ancestors had been stewards for centuries, was effectively off-limits to their family. Wu Tse's closest relatives moved away, scattering across the globe, and most of their property had been nationalized.

With no land, no dynasty can rule; with no heirs to pass on the family name, no dynasty can endure. What is a dynasty, if not name, and land?

We were seated in Wu Tse's dining room, beneath portraits of family members on the wall, including a striking man with a pyramid mustache she identified as her father, Edward, the last chieftain of Kokang. Wu Tse had lent me a copy of the book her eldest sister had written to make a record of the family history. "I only have the one copy; it's not something I can find again so easily," Wu Tse said, checking the pages before she went to slip it back onto its shelf in the book case.

The Yang family history is told in a series of upheavals and rebellions that each generation's ruler had to overcome. Olive appeared only fleetingly. Olive's rule and the family's inevitable loss of power that followed were given short shrift, characterized with reserved rancor. Olive was described as having unceremoniously taken power from her brother Edward until she was imprisoned—but was never described as having rebelled against him.

In the few years Olive was in charge, there were few advancements of the state of Kokang, but she had managed to earn a fortune with gambling and opium enterprises. Olive embodied every character flaw that led to the cultural awakening described in the prophetic poem and the dynasty's destruction.

Wu Tse was unwaveringly diplomatic when talking about Edward's deathbed regrets, but it was clearly a source of resentment among the siblings that Olive's turn at power had preceded their downfall.

"You know, a lot of things Olive did we shouldn't talk about; nobody wanted to talk about her. To be frank with you, we don't really talk about the past in the family—the painful memories. I don't like talking about it much either." It was not unusual for the families of purged leaders to inherit a reflexive secrecy about any sort of activity that could get them jailed. Wu Tse had an incredibly skillful friendly way of dodging every question I had before there was a chance to ask it.

"Do you think Olive will talk to me about those things that aren't in the book? Like how she got power from her brother, or if she worked for the CIA?"

"Many people have tried and failed," Wu Tse said, trying to dissuade me, listing people she'd refused to meet. At one point, even the CIA station chief had asked and been refused. "At the time, after she came out of Insein Prison, Olive was terrified of being arrested and never wanted to go back."

The authorities had watched Olive for decades. There had been spies posted at the street-side tea shop near her house, watching her every move and reporting every visitor to her house. She knew how to lay low and keep herself from becoming a target. Silence throughout the years had perhaps been what kept her alive.

"Olive has to be careful," Wu Tse said.

Disappointment spread across my face.

"Why don't you talk to Olive's sister, Judy." Wu Tse suggested she could use a visitor and was extremely talkative.

"I don't really talk to her, but maybe she will talk to you. She doesn't have much to do during the day now that she's retired so you won't be a nuisance to her."

JUDY

Olive's closest living sibling was her youngest, went by the English name Judy, and had been described to me as a rotund and hot-tempered schoolmarm with a penchant for gambling. At seventy-six, she had already outlived several husbands—though her siblings claimed it was more like she had worn them out.

Her cluttered ground-floor apartment was on a street in Sanchaung township in Yangon, with a pagoda at one end and a market at the other, connected by a narrow artery that became clogged with school children after lunchtime. Her front room was open to the street like a garage with a gate instead of a door, allowing the din of life from the street to drift in.

When I rapped the padlock against the metal like a knocker, a maid came to let me in while Judy slowly roused herself from the plastic chair where she had been waiting for me. She looked unexpectedly slight and moved very slowly. She wore her hair short and hadn't fully buttoned her threadbare blouse.

"I thought you would be a convent girl," she said, as she offered me a seat in a faded green plastic chair. Her visitors were normally old students from St. John's, a convent and high school where she had been an English teacher.

"So Wu Tse told you to meet me because she doesn't want to talk to you, she is fobbing you off on me, isn't that right?" Judy said and giggled, correctly assessing her relative's reticence to speak to me. "How did you know about my sister?"

"I heard your sister was a great military leader," I suggested, tentatively, unsure how she would respond to the characterization, given how little Wu Tse was willing to broach those subjects. The last thing I wanted to do was alienate Judy before I even had a chance to ask her if she could introduce me to Olive.

"My sister, the great Olive Yang, was once the bravest in the jungle, she wasn't afraid of anybody, and everybody feared her. Not even the police dared to arrest her. That is the

Figure 5.1. Judy Win pictured at her home in 2015.
GABRIELLE PALUCH.

true story about my sister. She is the kingmaker," Judy declared proudly, much to my relief.

Judy assumed a conspiratorial, forward-leaning stance. "You know what they say, if you dare cross her she will dare to have you killed!" she said, mimicking the sound of a gun, and then began to laugh as she watched the shock spread across my face.

"Don't worry, Gabby, I do not think she killed anybody. Not that I saw," Judy said and then amended the statement. "Never without a good reason."

The sound of a leaking drainpipe suddenly grew louder in the silence that followed. I wasn't shocked to hear that Olive would kill someone, but it was still unexpected to see an old woman so frail talk so casually about her sister being a murderer.

"We never want to talk about Olive, just now that you're asking me. Nobody wants to talk about Olive; there is nothing pleasant in her. Not many people here know I am a Yang or about my sister," she said, gesturing out toward the neighborhood just beyond her door.

"Why not?" I asked.

"Trouble, trouble, Olive is always trouble, always going here and there. My sister, always getting into trouble gallivanting with bad people. All the things we don't like, she will do. Olive even lost all our land," Judy said.

We were seated between a broken exercise bike and a plastic lawn chair across from a long wooden bench, piled high with newspapers and boxes, at which she cast a resentful gaze. She saw her sister's fitful reign as the final and emphatic exclamation point marking the dynasty's demise and her financial ruin.

"You know what they say,"—Judy began nearly every sentence this way—"the Yang family used to rule all of Kokang, but now we don't own even a stone," Judy was still smiling, though bitterly now.

"Are you talking about the family curse?" I asked.

"Curse? Olive is the curse!" she exclaimed, raising her voice in agitation, suddenly growing angry. "How can I love a sister who does all the bad things like giving away money, making me poor, that is true. Going in and out of jail all the time, and all the rubbish!"

"But she's still your sister, so you love her," I suggested. We sat across from one another in the narrow room, and I leaned forward to hear her better. It was hot, despite the fan that spun lazily in a corner, and sweat collected in the crease of my elbow.

"She never did anything good, how can I love a cheat? *Ashouq deh beh!*" she said, referring to her sister as "nothing but troublesome" in Burmese. When Judy was emphatic she would spit her words.

She continued to list more reasons to dislike her sister, taking pleasure in recounting all Olive's wrongdoings and unsavory associates.

"All these men like Lo Hsing Han, they are all rich because of my sister. If not for Olive, Lo Hsing Han would be nothing. He once followed Olive around to carry her cigarettes for her, and look now how he died a rich man. He betrayed my family, and now I'm poor."

"Are you upset with him?" I prodded.

"How can I like him? He is a drug dealer, I'm a school teacher, we are opposites. That's why I'm living in a shabby house." Judy looked at me like I was an idiot. "If I were a drug dealer I'd be riding a BMW in the city. I'm poor but happy. My conscience is clear, and I don't have to be afraid of anybody. I can go about. I'm not living surrounded by soldiers."

I found it hard to argue with what sounded like a very reasonable position for Judy to take on her sister's sordid criminal associates.

"All the followers in her army, she helped them and so they love her, but they can also betray her." Judy explained that Olive had built up a vast bank of favors among the most powerful members of the underworld in the Golden Triangle, and she had managed to survive by cashing in on those for decades.

"And Olive will do what she is not supposed to do—anything bad, she will do it." Judy said.

I started to visit Judy almost daily, in the late mornings before lunch, sometimes just to say hello. She had endearing ways of speaking: when she talked about Olive going to jail, she said she was "four-twenty," referring to the section of the Burmese penal code officers cited for an arrest. And she had a habit of telling me not to be late by saying, "Don't leave me waiting and lonesome."

Whenever I left Judy's apartment I would ask her what her plans were for the rest of the day as I prepared my things to leave. She always answered in the same way. "Gallivanting in a trishaw. I'll go here and there, see what is what." Judy assured me she always had fun gallivanting and liked to come home with snacks.

Judy wanted to know who I was dating and how much money I earned. She would admire my wallet and count the money inside. Sometimes she would remind me that it was customary to give elders gifts of money as a sign of respect.

"When people go to see Olive they give money, too. Olive always knows someone who can lend her money," she said.

During one visit, she angrily told me I was too young to know anything, and I didn't "know shit." At first, I was offended, but then her face softened, and she continued with a devilish smile, and said: "You should bring me diapers next time."

Figure 5.2. Judy Kyi Win, May 2015, pictured gallivanting in a trishaw near her home in Sanchaung, Yangon. GABRIELLE PALUCH.

Because she complained frequently about the price of adult incontinence products, I obligingly brought her a pack of diapers from the pharmacy around the corner the next day. I was worried she would be insulted, but they were met with genuine gratitude.

I tried all the questions I had for Olive on Judy. Did Olive smoke opium? *Rarely*. What did she get in trouble for? *Gallivanting*. How did she get paid for opium? *Guns and gold bars*. How did she end up in jail? *That depends which time*. Who was her greatest love? *Money*. Why did Olive name her son Jeep? *Because she missed her jeep car*. Who were her most hated enemies? *Communists and her husband*.

Every time I asked Judy if she would introduce me to Olive, she would tell me another story about her sister. She was like a repository for things people in the family didn't like to talk about.

"She almost stabbed a baby," Judy told me one day, out of the blue. She explained to me that it happened by mistake because Olive had suddenly pulled out a pocket knife while arguing with an uncle. Then, there was the time she almost shot her brother over a girl.

"Almost shot him?" I asked. Apparently just almost. Olive had just wanted to scare him, not kill him.

Most of Judy's ire centered around the belief that Olive had humiliated the family by insisting on being gay and squandering all the family's wealth on buying the affections of women who did not love her back. She often angrily repeated that she was poor and her sister had impoverished her, so now she could no longer play mahjong.

"She is not normal. She is what you call a lesbian. It's her nature, she was born that way, she likes girls, and she always does what she wants to do." Judy explained that Olive was compulsively falling in love with all the women who surrounded her, whether they were gay or not.

"Olive is always looking for love in the wrong places, she wants to be loved by everybody, even in her old age, she still wants to be loved, but they never love her, just want her money," Judy said, taking a tone of pity for her sister.

"What happened to all her money?" I asked.

"All spent!" Judy cried furiously, "all spent on houses for women, and I have to go see her in jail, such a lot of trouble she gives me and with this Wah Wah Win Shwe, all on my head."

I was shocked to hear that Wah Wah Win Shwe—the veritable Elizabeth Taylor of Burmese cinema—had such a shameful past. Wah Wah was a woman who blew kisses to adoring fans in the society pages of the newspapers.

"You mean Wah Wah put her in jail?"

"Put her in jail and took her house!" Judy shouted and then went on to list the names of Olive's love conquests. Judy named her brothers' girlfriends and her generals' wives; her prison warden but also her live-in maids; and a legendary beauty queen.

"Did Olive love her husband?"

"Not her husband! She hated him, she didn't want to be married, she didn't want to have sex with him, so then they had a big fight after," Judy said, mimicking punching and kicking.

Judy was of a generation of women who were unfamiliar with the concept of marital rape. She had been taught that a woman had the duty to bear children, so being forced into marriage and childbirth was a matter of course.

"Was Olive raped?" I asked.

"It wasn't rape; she just didn't want to have sex with him. It was a legal marriage," Judy said, unaware of how the contradiction she had just spoken would land on my ears. Then she added for specificity, "a legal marriage with her cousin."

Olive's son had been the product of what I had been taught to recognize as incestuous marital rape—but to Judy, this was a completely unremarkable detail. Judy speculated that the repeated intermarriage between the two families was what had made Olive's son come out so odd.

"She hated being pregnant, she didn't want to be a mother. And then she left to go live with the bandits. Olive always does that, go here and there. You know what they say, she never took care of her son. Olive was never there."

The fateful decision Olive made to abandon married life and take control of an army to engage in banditry against the family's wishes had been portrayed to me repeatedly as an inexplicably bold-faced power grab; what the *Dim Light* would call an act of overwhelming selfishness.

To Judy, Olive was the vilified embodiment of the curse that afflicted the whole family, and so she could not understand what motivated Olive to leave her husband.

But given Olive never wanted to be married, it now seemed more like the type of decision made out of desperation to escape a husband who would almost certainly rape her again.

"So that's why she went to live with the bandits? Because she didn't want to be with her husband and son?" I asked.

"Yes, that's why she is always going with the bad people and going to jail instead of taking care of her son. I already told you Gabby, Olive is no good. She does all the bad things a person can do," Judy said.

I had grown used to leaving Judy's apartment in a state of shock, but when I let myself out that day, I was crestfallen. I had heard the stories about little baby Olive, and I had heard the stories of the violent and fearsome Miss Hairy Legs who rose to power as a hero among bandits. But in between, Olive was a hero to herself in a way that nobody else around her understood—and her sister even hated her for it.

So I was incensed a few days later when I suddenly learned Olive would rest for eternity alongside the man she had escaped. There were plans for Olive's tomb to be built in none other than her ex-husband's family grounds.

It was a perfectly cloudless day when Wu Tse took me along to the cemetery just north of her house to pay respects to her father's grave.

We walked past rows of exquisite tombs covered in Chinese poetry and elegies that glinted in the bright sun, and it struck me as odd that Edward wouldn't be buried in Kokang, along with his ancestors. "Why is Edward here?" I asked, as we approached a grouping of well-kept shrines.

"Well he was buried up in Lashio, but it became too difficult to go pay respects every year," Wu Tse said, explaining that as the seasonal fighting between various militias in the region had surged and waned over the years, they wanted to have him closer by so they wouldn't have to weigh safety risks against the obligation to their ancestors.

The decision hadn't been taken lightly to move the grave. Unearthing the casket had been a punishingly painstaking process when they moved the bones all the way down to Yangon from Lashio. "We had to do it even though it's not the tradition to separate a ruler so far from his land."

It had been more than two decades since Wu Tse had visited the ancestors in Kokang, the place to which their family name belongs.

"We were supposed to go this year but then the fighting happened so we're glad he is here," Wu Tse said, gesturing toward Edward's tomb. Then, she pointed to another grave nearby facing Edward's. It was Lo Hsing Han's.

"It's by coincidence they're so close, because they put all the Kokang people together in one section in the cemetery; Edward was already here when he died," Wu Tse explained, with a smile that indicated the irony was not lost on her.

Edward, having been extracted from his land, was entombed across from the traitor who ousted their family and then rose to riches with an empire of his own. How fitting the two rivals would continue to face one another in death.

Wu Tse took a moment to fold her hands and bow, then did the same at her mother's tomb which was just next to it. When she had finished paying respects, she swept around the graves and made sure they looked tidy.

"It's very sad but this is the way it is for us now. Not even Olive will be buried in Kokang," Wu Tse said, as we continued walking, that instead of being laid to rest alongside Yang rulers, Olive would eventually be interred on her husband's ancestral burial ground, near where she lived with her stepson. "I guess it's right for the husband's family, and a husband should be buried with his wife," she concluded.

"Wouldn't Olive prefer to be in Kokang?" I asked, surprised. Olive had endured great pain to be separated from her husband, and to defend her autonomy in her ancestral homeland—now in death she would be alongside a husband she never wanted in the ground that wasn't hers.

"Probably yes, but it's too dangerous with all the fighting," Wu Tse said. But the plan had been laid in stone: the granite tomb had already been partially built, arranged, and paid for.

"Perhaps Olive's stepson would show me?" I asked, hoping to learn more about the man who had turned me away in Muse.

"Not even I like to talk to him. I don't want to know, to be honest." Wu Tse laughed uncomfortably, covering her mouth. Wu Tse made a point of staying out of their business—for her own safety. When Olive had decided to move up there, she was sad not to see much of her anymore, but it was just too dangerous. "Olive is safe there, and that's what matters."

CHAPTER SIX

Operation Paper and the Queen of Kokang

SECRET ARMY SOLDIERS WHO RETURNED FROM THE FRONT ROMANTICIZED Olive as their own Joan of Arc when they told of her bravery as a fallen hero who sacrificed her life in the name of the anti-communist cause.

When her tiny body clung to a majestic white horse, deftly navigating the treacherous hills at high speeds with her whip, there were always at least eight followers on horseback in her wake. Her double-holstered belt sat atop trousers, and her American army jacket on top of that. She wore the Secret Army's hallmark red scarf across her face.

After withdrawing from the failed invasion of China, hurrahs rose from the wounded brothers when they saw their beloved heroine galloping into their anti-communist base. They whooped and cheered when she shot her pair of guns, felling two coconuts from a palm so far away, they hadn't seen them until they dropped.

But not even her military fashion could blind them to her feminine gifts.

An army captain lying in a stretcher under the sparse shade of a coconut palm was taken by her rosy, baby skin, her big eyes, and sisterly manner. Miss Yang's teeth were so pearly, he told her he thought she was an American movie actress playing a guerilla soldier, not an actual soldier.

"I'm but a wild girl," she said. She would hear none of his compliments. Instead, she wanted to talk to him about his pretty, silky-haired wife, who had become a close friend.

Miss Yang was indignant she had been left behind during the invasion: what she truly desired was to be commander-in-chief of a column of soldiers.

So, to appease her, just a few months later, she was given the title of Commander of the Fourth Column of independent guerillas. Olive brazenly tried to prove herself in battle, leading troops on horseback on a starry night on the banks of the Salween River.

But her courage proved foolhardy, and after the legendary battle during which so many men were lost, Miss Yang was never seen again. Her courageous self-sacrificing character had gained the admiration of an entire army after risking life and reputation for others in a moment of need.

The captain feared to imagine what slaughter had been Olive's fate, when he never learned exactly what happened to her, so merciless were the Burmese.

Heaven had bestowed such a heavy load—saving the country and people—onto such a weak, unmarried woman. They prayed for their fellow warrior, their heroine. "God, God do bless her!"

When the Secret Army officers spoke of Miss Yang, they saw no manly hearted menace: they hailed her as their singular "Joan of Arc!"[1]

Sometime before the end of 1950, not far from the 101 garrison, Olive had the anguishing experience of giving birth to a child she didn't want to have. The day Jeep came into the world was a day nobody bothered to remember and tell him about later, and so he was never sure when exactly his real birthday was.

A story Olive's siblings like to tell is that Olive was so angry after delivery that she could not bear to hear the baby's crying voice, and he was sent away. Kokang at the time had no hospitals, only midwives and wet-nurses. So when Olive refused to allow her baby near her chest to breastfeed, even in the moments after birth, the baby was calmed by an attendant instead. When a distraught post-natal Olive was asked what to call the new baby son, Olive had a ready, touching answer: Jeep.

Olive bought her first American Jeep on the black market in Kunming. Olive's mother had been riding in the British Consul's saloon car that was easily waved through any checkpoints because of its diplomatic markings. Olive intended to take the jeep back to Kokang and painted a British flag on her door to fool police into allowing her to pass easily through checkpoints on the way. But the plan almost immediately backfired: as soon as she drove to visit her mother at the Consulate, it was confiscated.

Olive had always loved that car and regretted that it had been taken away from her. So when her son arrived, she called him Jeep. In his infancy, Jeep grew to love the woman who nursed him and doted on him lovingly in Olive's frequent lengthy absences. She took pity on Jeep, who began to regard her as his mother instead.

And when Olive reemerged after giving birth, she had undergone a remarkable outward transformation since leaving her husband, of which people took note.

Olive's girlish shoulder-length hair was now cropped like a man's. Olive had a feminine figure, but now with breasts bound there were few outward indicators that Olive was born into a woman's body. Olive, dressed in fatigues, working as a caravan trader, was easy to mistake for a man from afar.

Olive had started talking a little differently. Wherever she went, she would strike up conversation by saying, "I'm thinking about joining the resistance."

Then Olive would turn to anybody who was around, and say, "How about you? What do you think?"

Thousands more of Generalissimo Chiang's men who escaped the communists plundered their way across the Burmese countryside looking for food and shelter. They established a base in a remote mountainous area of Shan State near the border with Thailand and they eventually started calling themselves the Secret Army.

After a Burmese fighter pilot with backward-mounted rockets shot himself out of the sky during a rogue mission to attack them, they claimed to have downed the plane themselves with rifles. Then they reached an agreement with the relatively new Burma Army commander-in-chief General Ne Win, who allowed them to stay.[2]

The first Secret Army scouts who met Olive thought she was beautiful and began to tell her of their plans. Their general commander proclaimed the admittedly quixotic intention of taking back mainland China and had reassured Olive of General Chennault's support for the planned invasion of Yunnan and the resistance against the communists.[3] Nobody knew what the CIA was, but General Chennault's name was as good as gold, because his planes had been at the vanguard of their liberation in World War II.

"I'll come with a few hundred men," Olive said, confident she could gather followers. "But first, I'd like to meet the commander."

Rumors got around that the Secret Army was offering new American weapons to soldiers who pledged to join the conquest of Yunnan. A fugitive known as the Ponytailed Bandit showed up—his hair reached to his waist and was said to protect him from evil. He was wanted for murder by the Chinese communist officials who snuck in and was looking for arms for his band of forty.

Soon, every bandit in Kokang started to join the resistance. Kokang was too hilly for an airbase, but the 101 garrison was perfectly situated for an intelligence outpost and even still had some old radio equipment that badly needed repairing. There was just one problem: they needed more men.[4]

Olive set out that August, traveling southward with eight men and three pack mules along the road from her husband's village, where they had been recruiting more followers. Traveling in Shan State in 1950 was extremely treacherous: There were free-roaming rebels, and bandits were so desperate they would rob the pants off you.[5]

Ever since the Secret Army had turned up, police had been arresting Chinese-speakers around those parts just for good measure, so Olive had to be careful. As the twilight turned to darkness on the fourth night of their journey, they were approaching a small hamlet, where they planned to spend the night before continuing on.

When Olive and the entourage went to announce themselves to the village headman as was customary for travelers, he wasn't home. Thinking that was a bit odd, they checked the village hall nearby, in case there was something going on there.

Instead of the village headman, Olive found two exceedingly officious, unfamiliar Burmese men in uniform smelling of liquor. It was rare Olive encountered unfamiliar people in these parts.

"Name!" They demanded Olive identify herself, but Olive was not used to having to explain who she was.[6] She hated that more than being disrespected or bullied by people who didn't know better.

"I've just come from across the river with my attendants and employees," Olive explained, annoyed. "And who are you?"

The Burmese officers refused to answer and continued to press Olive with questions.

"And why would a woman be traveling alone along these unsafe roads?" they asked, sizing her up, confused by her clothing. "Why would a woman be dressed like that?"

The officers were behaving in a way Olive found unnecessarily rude, in fact, nothing short of threatening.

"You aren't cooperating with rebels, are you?" the officers suggested,[7] before attempting to exact bribes. "For 300 Rupees you can continue on."

Olive was certain that something wasn't quite right as she began to assess the situation from a strategic perspective. Her eyes darted around the village hall, and she noticed figures huddled in the next room—they were the family members of the village chief.

Olive was indignant, surely the officers had bullied the village chief, and thought shaking down a ragged-looking bunch like them would be easy. She was certain that she and her men could handle the drunkards, who had no sense who they were dealing with. Olive dug in her heels: she knew of no rule or fine that justified their demand.

"You have no reason to squeeze any money from me," Olive said, just as her eight-man rank-and-file walked through the door behind her.

It was unclear who started it, but a brawl ensued. One of the officers, the shorter one, leapt to attack Olive. Her followers sprang into action, quickly subduing the officers until they tied them up with rope, battered and bloody.

The way Olive told the story, the chieftain's family emerged from hiding, cheering Olive's bravery. "Don't worry, these men won't bother you anymore!" Olive promised, as Olive's followers loaded the potentially vengeful cops onto their mules.

They rode on through the night, all the way east, to the nearest ferry crossing into Kokang. Once they got to the edge of their territory,[8] Olive released the prisoners and then escaped across to safety, where they knew the Burmese would be too scared to follow and had no legal authority to arrest them. They gave them a few hundred Rupees so they wouldn't squeal, roughly equivalent to the bribe they had demanded in the first place.[9]

It wasn't until four months later, when Edward returned from a trip to the United States, that he learned Olive had absconded from her husband's court, declared herself divorced, and given birth. Edward was away on urgent government business attending the United Nations General Assembly in New York.

The officers who brawled with Olive returned from their captivity only to tell the assistant resident, who filed a report of complaint to the Kokang administrative offices.

"You were kidnapped?" the assistant resident noted down for his report, horrified, "and you say she was neither man nor woman?"

Repeated, frantic inquiries regarding the incident involving the woman dressed in men's clothes who had kidnapped Burmese officers were ignored.

Edward's deputy had insisted it was a case of mistaken identity, given Olive's unusual mode of dress. Since Olive was easily mistaken for a man, surely they had seen someone else riding on to the rebel trading posts.

Edward was incensed. Armed kidnapping was illegal. Olive insisted she had done nothing wrong but stand up for herself. Everywhere they went, Burmese officials were exacting bribes from them because they looked Chinese, and it wasn't fair. They had started it by harassing her, not the other way around. Edward scolded his sister for carelessly getting in trouble while traveling around on the treacherous roads, counseling her to go back home and stay out of trouble.

"The incident was a great misunderstanding," Olive told Sao Hom Hpa when she was finally asked to appear in his court.

Sao Hom Hpa was used to Olive's excuses and had heard about the beautiful bandit on a white stallion, seen together with the Kachin insurgents who robbed his bank. "Have you been colluding with bandits?"

"Never!" Olive insisted. "In fact, I returned to Kokang immediately upon hearing of the presence of people who were disloyal to the government!"

Figure 6.1.   Edward Yang pictured at the yamen, the family court in Kyadiling, ca. 1941, shortly before it was burned by Japanese troops. YANG FAMILY PRIVATE COLLECTION.

In the letter of apology she was compelled to write that day, Olive said she felt very ashamed for her behavior and regretted kidnapping the officers.

Finally, she emphasized at the end of her letter, her denial of any cooperation with any sort of rebel forces, communist or otherwise, of which she may have been accused. "I can definitely say that I have no sort of connection or any concern with them," she wrote.

Olive promised that she would from now on remain home in Kokang. Despite Edward's vows to keep a watchful eye on his sister, Olive did no such thing.[10]

That February, the first CIA stocks of weapons that would eventually reach Olive began their voyage by ship. The CIA now co-owned Chennault's airline, headquartered in a picturesque oceanside town on the island of Taiwan. Chennault had planned the operation personally together with the Secret Army's commander at a compound where hundreds of American personnel were training guerillas, providing logistical support.[11]

Money was finally made available to Chennault for Operation Paper through the CIA after President Harry Truman personally approved $5 million against the best advice of numerous advisors, including the CIA director himself. Plans were never detailed in any Pentagon Papers, because it was so heavily classified. The first incursion was intended to be a diversionary attack to the war in Korea.[12]

The cargo was declared as twenty tons of "pineapple, tea, and camphor powder" destined for SEA Supply, the CIA's front company in Bangkok. What was in fact weapons, ammunition, and radio equipment traveled by train to the Secret Army headquarters in Chiang Mai, manned by an officer who went by the alias "Mr. Ho." A specially trained Thai counterinsurgency force escorted the weapons with a US delegation to the Burmese border.[13]

At the border crossing, a Secret Army caravan of several dozen mules showed up to hand over a large amount of opium in exchange for the weapons. Two SEA Supply employees, operations and radio officers for Chennault's airline who spoke some Mandarin, helped load the weapons, radio sets, and ammunition onto mules. Then they saddled up themselves for the eighty-mile journey to the new Secret Army base back in Burma, in a town called Mong Hsat.[14]

Olive knew the roads and trails around Mong Hsat well and would later in her old age tell her caretaker of journeys along this fabled route. The arrival of the weapons and the two Americans —who were reportedly slightly wimpy and arrogant, though efficient—was highly anticipated in Mong Hsat. They immediately got to work on repairs needed to receive future weapons from Chennault's planes by airdrop at the dilapidated old air base built during World War II.

That March, Edward unveiled the monument to Kokang's fallen heroes of World War II, on the exact spot his younger brother had been shot in the mutiny. The veterans honored that day were given land and appointed as village headmen. Then Edward moved to Lashio to take his new position as minister, leaving his relatives in charge to report to the new Burmese government official assigned to their region.[15]

When the new Burmese assistant resident reported to his post that year, he spoke no Chinese, and none of the family administrators seemed to be available to help him translate. When he tried to find a building for his headquarters or residence, none of the war-veteran headmen were willing to rent him a house, so he had to stay in a town across the ferry. His quarters were so small he was forced to live together with his staff in an office.

To make matters worse, the assistant resident had heard about the fearsome murderous bandits roaming the border, of and the chieftain's sister, who had a masculine personality and kidnapped people. So without the escort of an armed guard, he was too afraid to take his post, and they had foiled his attempts to station a police officer in Kokang. He had resigned himself to the idea of administering a state he could not enter and relied on painstakingly translated reports from Edward to know what was going on.[16]

At a rally at the Secret Army's base in Mong Hsat, superiors from Taiwan came to inspire beloved soldiers of the revolution to fulfill their secret mission before the invasion of Yunnan.[17]

"For your own sakes, for the nation," they were told Generalissimo Chiang himself had sent word, "struggle through all the hardship, for the winning of the final victory of resistance against communism!"

But after the special banquet for senior officers from Taiwan and the two American radio operators, the Secret Army commander privately confided his true intentions to his deputy: the majority of their new recruits would stay behind during the liberation of Yunnan.[18]

"Once the weapons are delivered, the regiments will man our bases," the Secret Army commander explained. The main purpose of attacking Yunnan was to get the promised weapons deliveries from the Americans and expand their force.[19]

In some exaggerated tellings of the story, Olive was there for the legendary parade of the Secret Army troops at their training base before they launched their invasion of Yunnan. And in one telling that is almost certainly invented, as soon as Olive learned she would not invade China, she angrily galloped the entire eighty miles to Thailand without stopping. Then, as revenge, she seduced the Secret Army Commander's wife with nothing more than flattery and a cowrie shell comb for her hair.

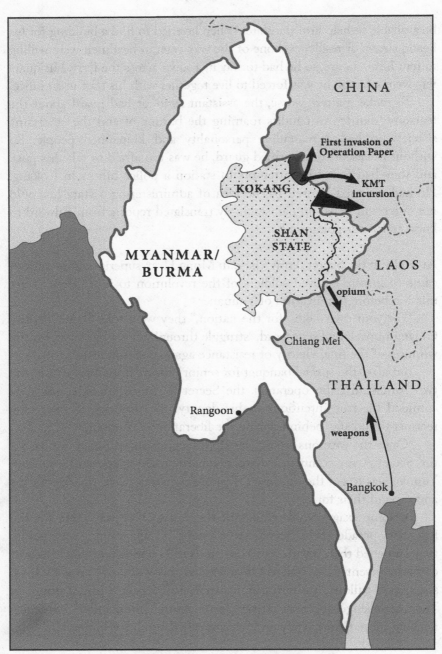

Map 6.1.   The first Secret Army (Kuomintang) Incursion

The two-thousand-man Secret Army attack force and mules arduously marched up the Salween River toward their staging bases in wild Wa State. They would have to cross Savage Mountain to reach the target for their invasion.[20] Secret Army men knew of the terrifying dangers that lurked there, like the toxic miasma that rose from the mimosa weeds and left men dead in their tracks. Some had already survived harrowing ambushes by naked savages, and it was well-known that to enter any Wa village, one had to either be invited or fight.

Right in the heart of Savage Mountain, they say it was Olive who convinced the Wa chieftain to allow them to establish a base in a town called Mongmao.[21] Olive rode down from Kokang to join the Secret Army, together with Fat Huang, the Ponytailed Bandit. Between the three of them, they had a gang of about three hundred thieves.[22] They quickly set up a training camp and cleared a drop zone. The Americans with them had radios, and soon the first airdrops of weapons and supplies came in, falling from the unmarked Dakotas overhead.

The Secret Army commander began distributing boxes of American rifles to Wa headhunters whose weaponry traditionally consisted of long-bladed knives known as *dahs*, spears, and crossbows. Using bamboo poles as dummies on a shooting range, the two Americans began to teach the Wa warriors to shoot the new modern weapons with the best effect at the firing line and how to capture the most valuable war materials from opponents.[23] There were rations of corned beef and even brand new shoes and American uniforms with pocketed shirts.

They set out under Generalissimo Chiang's blue banner with the white sun, in the predawn darkness at the staging base in late May of 1951, believing the oppressed masses across the border would rise up and join them to overthrow their new communist overlords. Within fifty days hundreds of them had died while trying to invade China.

General Li led a coordinated advance staged from the 101 garrison in Kokang, entering the neighboring county in China without resistance. He briefly succeeded in setting up a government, and nearly two thousand men submitted themselves to his rule. Over the first week in June, the Americans directed Dakotas that dropped rifles, carbines, ammunition, as well as fourteen paratroopers.[24] Olive and the Ponytailed Bandit with a few hundred men gallivanted across the countryside behind them, looting homes, grain stores, and robbing hundreds of cattle.[25]

Congratulations were telegraphed to several senior officers, and promised salaries were distributed based on the admittedly outrageous claim to have twenty thousand troops. But they never advanced beyond there. The detachment of Wa warriors began an advance on a strategic airfield the Secret Army intended to seize. Just eighteen miles short of the target, thousands of communist troops blocked vanguard Secret Army columns, and the Wa militiamen absorbed the brunt of a vicious counterattack, killing hundreds of them.[26]

The Secret Army commander led at least another thousand men in attacks elsewhere to similar effect. By the time his detachments confronted the enemy, they had used most of their ammunition, so after just two days of halfhearted fighting, they lost all positions and soon devolved into a general retreat back to Burma.[27]

Several of the CIA's advisors and paratroopers were killed. The two American radio operators narrowly escaped death during their evacuation, when their helicopter had mechanical trouble. They had to light the aircraft on fire before abandoning it, retreating overland with troops before continuing on to Bangkok.[28]

The Secret Army commander was undeterred. From a little Baptist church back in Burma, he perhaps somewhat delusionally appointed himself the president of Yunnan in exile, commissioned more Wa tribal leaders, and prepared for another attack. They were no match for Chinese artillery during the second invasion, which was equally disastrous for their warriors.[29]

Countless were injured and required medical attention as they humiliatingly retreated to their base. Those who were lucky enough to survive the invasion were in bad shape as they made their way back into Burma. There were several desertions and a few disturbing suicides. Olive's caravan distributed the loot at their base, rice and medical supplies dropped by the Dakotas.[30]

After just a few days of rest, a regiment of Burmese troops started an advance, hoping to drive the foreign invaders from their territory in their moment of weakness. So the Secret Army commander made plans to evacuate.

"Move in, like a dove occupies a magpie's nest!" The Secret Army commander told his men, meaning they were to insinuate themselves into local society by marrying local women. The Secret Army Commander had been told Olive was a strongheaded woman who was not interested in marrying, so instead, she was given a titular role in exchange for allowing some of the surviving warriors safe haven in Kokang. Then the Secret Army commander appointed Fat Huang and the Ponytailed Bandit as his generals under Olive.[31]

He told them to get themselves to Kokang, where a beautiful maiden on a white horse awaited to help those in need.

Those who heard Olive was merciful streamed into the family court in Old Street Village. The several hundred Secret Army troops marched on narrow trails through numerous villages across Kokang, and could not possibly have gone unnoticed. Because the Burmese resident assistant wasn't there to stop them, they proceeded undisturbed. Among them was a group of about eight hundred Was, having defected from China.[32]

Some of the men went to a garrison with the Ponytailed Bandit, some with Fat Huang. And some of General Li's men went to the only two remaining villages of Kokang's original inhabitants, the Hke Hpok people who were particularly well-known for opium cultivation and began to set up camp.[33]

Judy said people who came to Olive looking for help were not normal people. Some of them wanted to marry Olive. Some of them had previously worked as house-slaves and never left their villages before. They prostrated themselves, as was customary in the family court. Among the grateful, battle-weary who eventually went to see Olive was a captain and Taiwanese intelligence agent known as the Borderland Poet, who memorialized her in a poetic couplet:

The Queen of Old Street became like a celestial fairy, her smile
spreading cheek-to-cheek
Guerillas bowed down. The beautiful woman from the mountaintop,
praised their persistence.[34]

Shortly thereafter Sao Hom Hpa summoned Edward for an urgent meeting in his court in Lashio.

"There's a Chinese infiltration in your garrisons." Sao Hom Hpa told Edward about the Secret Army soldiers who had occupied nearly all of central Kokang, taking over fields, and the escaping farmers who had trickled into his villages.[35]

"Our men have been instructed to shoot armed intruders on sight, there's communists everywhere," Edward insisted. His subordinates would have informed him of any such infiltration, they were simply fending off communists.

"I have to protect my borders," Sao Hom Hpa told Edward. He saw Kokang as a lost cause and didn't want to be blamed for it. So he ended their military partnership.[36]

A few weeks later at the War Office in Rangoon, the defense minister made a fateful and unusual decision that left the Kokang military command and budget entirely under the Yang family's control. While all the other chieftain's militias were absorbed into the Burmese military police, Edward's Kokang Self-Defense Force was kept on as a Chinese-speaking unit under Kokang command and disbursed a special block grant to the Yang family's administrative office. The Kokang Self-Defense Force was now an independent volunteer guerilla force designed to fight the ongoing Chinese infiltration around Kokang— under Edward's remote supervision.[37]

The way Judy told the story, the infamous incident during which Olive nearly accidentally stabbed a baby happened some time after that. Olive was over the moon, telling everybody in Old Street Village the Secret Army commander had personally appointed her as queen-commander of the region, to fight the impending invasion of the communists.

Their Uncle Charlie, left in charge at the family court, tried to talk sense into Olive and impress upon her that joining the Secret Army was illegal. They got into a frightening argument.

"Edward could lose his seat in parliament," Uncle Charlie admonished Olive. "You can't go around talking like you're a commander like that."

For Olive, who had been repeatedly told from a young age, she couldn't be a general because she wasn't a man, this struck a chord.

"The communists are planning an invasion, and we are the guardians of the frontier," Olive began and pulled out a knife intending to emphasize her martial ability by skillfully sticking it into the wall. In an uncharacteristically clumsy moment, Olive mistakenly stuck the blade in the leg of their uncle's daughter, who was coincidentally cradling her new-born baby nearby. Blood gushed forth.

"I didn't mean it! I'm sorry!" Olive cried, horrified at the wound and the crying baby.

"Better just stay out of her way," her cousin said quietly to her father, as Olive rushed out of the house to fetch a nearby midwife to care for the injury. Ever since their father had died, Olive was impossible to control.

While Olive had been gallivanting around Kokang, down in Rangoon in his stately new home near the lake, Jimmy was unnerved by news about a possible communist invasion. of Burma through Kokang: one thousand Chinese Communist Party men had arrived at Kokang's borders, with the intention of claiming their Burmese land for China.[38] The unrest in Kokang had delayed Jimmy's day at the polls in the country's first general election, and his constituents remained some of the only people in the country still waiting to exercise their vote.[39]

Jimmy had gotten to know his neighbor across the lake, US Ambassador David Key, who seemed to have a cavalier attitude towards the communists. When he and Edward spoke to Ambassador Key, they tried to impress upon him how serious the situation had become, he seemed more curious about the Americans.

"There are four Americans with them, armed with the latest American weapons from Taiwan," Edward told Ambassador Key. As the highest ranking US diplomat in the country, if the CIA had planned operations, it was the sort of thing he should have known about. Earlier that year, he had caught wind that Americans had been gunrunning. Ambassador Key asked his superiors about the two Americans supplying anti-communist troops with modern American weapons. He was told they were Chennault's employees, and his request to cancel their passports was refused.[40]

The CIA's numerous shell companies did little to hide their involvement. That summer, a reporter identified and traced Chennault's aircraft to the disguised CIA offices in Bangkok, connecting the cargo to the Secret Army's commander.[41] Ambassador Key could easily see the hallmarks of a clandestine operation connected to the Chinese guerillas, which he suspected was being directed out of Thailand. But when Ambassador Key inquired with CIA officials there, they denied knowledge of the mission. Finally fed up, Ambassador Key sent a scathing cable to Washington in August 1951, excoriating their folly that had cost them heavily in terms of Burmese goodwill and trust. Ambassador Key publicly resigned over the matter.[42]

Nevertheless, a memo regarding another rebel offensive in Burma crossed President Harry Truman's desk. In the case that Burma fell to communists amassing at its borders, the CIA would activate cells of anti-communist guerillas, as a "third force" they hoped would form a buffer to contain communism inside China. The Secret Army commander distributed boxes of money to recruits at their base for another invasion shortly thereafter.[43]

CHAPTER SEVEN

The Olive Branch

JEEP

EVEN BEFORE I MET JEEP, THE STORIES JUDY HAD TOLD ME ABOUT HIS childhood made my heart ache.

I had been told his mother had foolishly left him for banditry, wealth, and a diva movie star, who didn't want him in the house. After having grown up fatherless, the wound of this betrayal had shrouded him in a perpetual state of longing and resentment, living alone in Thailand ever since his mother went to Insein Prison. The last letter he'd sent to his mother had arrived over ten years ago. Not even the cousins who had spent their early childhoods with Jeep knew where to find him. It had taken me nearly a year to find a way to reach him, and when I called, he was stunned.

"Did my mother send you?" he asked, after stuttering in shock.

I wondered how he knew.

Because he had a "special friend" visiting him on Sunday, he explained he wished to see me Saturday.

He lived in Chiang Mai, in a poorly maintained house with a wild, unkempt tropical garden that looked out of place next to the neatly trimmed hedges of his neighbors. A slight man who looked like a swarthy, sturdier version of Olive appeared at the door as soon as I arrived. He was, as promised, an unusual man and spoke with a harried affect that made it seem as though everything he was saying was in a rush to get out.

"Jeep?" I asked, as he welcomed me inside his home.

"Nobody calls me by that name here," he said, caught off guard by how it sounded. "That's why I agreed to meet you, because it's so nice to hear that name again. I never hear my name as my family says it."

He knew it was a little strange but liked it anyway. "Jeep" was both a name and a term of endearment: Olive loved Jeeps in particular, and he had been named after the first Jeep she had lost. When Jeep heard his name, he was reminded that he was precious to his mother.

As I approached him, and we greeted one another in the entryway, I noticed there were tears in his eyes, and his hands were shaking. He pointed to his reflection in a mirror on the wall.

"Every time I look at myself I see my mother," he remarked, as he discreetly wiped at his eyes with the back of his hand.

We walked through his house into a shaded part of the garden and sat in two weather-beaten lawn chairs alongside a canal brimming with lotus blossoms and littered with broken gardening equipment.

Jeep clearly missed Olive; but as soon as I asked him when they last spoke, his expression changed, and he claimed amnesia regarding his childhood.

"Why should I remember it if I have nothing there? They have forgotten me, so I have forgotten them. I'm a losing man! I'm a forgotten, losing man!" he cried out repeatedly, clearly pained by a memory he wished he didn't have.

He did, indeed, appear to have been forgotten from an early age. Olive demonstrated affection with money and gifts, like a traditional father but displayed none of the attentiveness of a mother. Jeep had grown up with his uncles, hearing stories of his mother's escapades and mischief, and how upset it made them. By the time he finally returned to Kokang together with his mother, he was afraid of her. Wherever they went together, he could tell other people were afraid of her, too. He hadn't been old enough to understand exactly why Olive was away, but he knew she was doing something bad.

Once Olive was gone in Insein Prison, Jeep's life turned to a series of increasingly traumatic displacements. When the Yang family was finally expelled from Kokang and fled on foot to Thailand, Jeep was just a fourteen-year-old boy, and everybody was trying their best to fend for themselves.

"I'm not like you, I don't have a university education," Jeep explained, bitterly. Jeep was together with his Uncle Jimmy, who had become the leader of their troops in Olive's absence, and the only familiar faces Jeep knew were the men in their army. Nobody forced him to join, but he didn't feel like he had a choice.

His voice shook with resentment as he cried out, "I was a child soldier!"

I tried not to let my surprise show. There was something particularly upsetting about the idea of Olive's son unwillingly following in his mother's footsteps without the benefits of her tutelage: As a child-conscript, Jeep had fallen victim to one of the very predations with which his mother was charged.

Jeep did not take to life as a soldier. He was uncomfortable carrying a gun and avoided any jobs around the base that could end in violence. Many of his mother's former men had been recruited as children, so Jeep felt guilty when he lived among them, because he was relatively lucky to have had any sort of education at all.

"So you didn't want to be a general, like your mom?" I asked.

"Fifty gangsters with guns in a village call themselves generals because they bully people around. Do you call that a general? You know the US has an aircraft carrier that holds one thousand sailors," Jeep retorted, pointedly. He had heated up and started describing the aircraft carrier at length.

"A person who commands that is a general."

After spending his teenage years between armed outposts with his Uncle Jimmy in Thailand, most of the people Jeep knew were trained mercenaries. One by one, they began disappearing.[1] Then, Uncle Jimmy was arrested. Jeep was terrified: He was stateless, broke, and alone. None of them had proper immigration papers. He went into hiding in the jungle but got sick of being afraid all the time after his cousin was assassinated by Lo Hsing Han's men.

Jeep didn't feel quite in place in Thailand; he couldn't go back home to Burma and certainly not back to Kokang. His mother was the only remaining relative to whom he felt connected there—but all this time he had never heard from her. He decided to become an English teacher in Chiang Mai instead.

"Now, I'm just waiting for my mother to die. You know, I could have gone back when my father died, but that time has passed. I left all that behind, all the dangerous people. If I were to go back, that would mean a war. That's why I make this sacrifice and stay in Thailand," Jeep said.

As Duan's firstborn son, Jeep could have been successor to the leadership of a lucrative and powerful militia with established ties to the national military. But the day of his father's death some decades ago, his father's second son and half-brother called him to ask if he intended to return to make a claim of succession. Jeep said he knew better than to say yes; he believed the invitation was surely a lure to fool him into walking into a planned assassination attempt that could trigger revenge killings.

He had good reason to believe he could never go back home: The last time he had dared visit his mother in Myanmar, something terrifying had happened.

Sometime in 2003, Jeep had received word that his mother was dying. They hadn't exchanged letters in decades, and he was shocked to see it in his mailbox. She'd suffered a heart attack, she wrote, and been in a coma. When she came to in the hospital, she'd wondered where Jeep was.

"I want to see my only flesh and blood before I die," Olive wrote, it had been too many years since they had laid eyes on one another. "Come visit in Rangoon."

Jeep had not been back in over thirty years. Immediately upon arrival at the airport, he was arrested by immigration authorities and taken to a holding cell. Nobody told him why. His mother, still recovering from her recent hospitalization, was desperately looking for him at the arrivals lounge. She had to call in a special favor to get him released. "When I finally saw her I just cried, and I cried, and I cried. My mother told me to be strong," he said.

Jeep vowed never to return.

"Not even for my mother's funeral, no way, not if he's there! There is nothing there for me. As soon as I enter the country they'll arrest me.

Before I even get on the plane in Bangkok they will know I'm coming, trust me, they'll know," Jeep said as though trying to convince me.

By the time he was back in Thailand, Jeep was convinced his mother had tried to recruit him into being her agent in Chiang Mai, and his half-brother had tried to scupper the deal.

So, Jeep wrote a letter to his mother. He sealed it in an envelope, pinned it to his wall and scrawled the date and the words "no more love" into the paint next to it.

Coincidentally on the way to the restroom as I was leaving the house I saw the wall-hanging in the hallway. It was so unusual, I asked him what was in the letter before I had a chance to think about how personal it must be.

"Oh, I could never say, I could never say. All of the things that I never told her."

I asked Jeep if he planned to ever send the letter, but he responded to a completely different question.

"You know you should really be more careful. My brother is a dangerous, lawless man, you should be afraid of him too, you may be raped or killed." He read the shock on my face and added, as if it would assuage me, "Don't worry, I cannot rape you, I'm too old now."

Then he showed me into the restroom. When I emerged, he escorted me out of the house and shook my hand firmly as he asked me to stay in touch.

"Please, be careful with yourself," he reminded me with sincerity.

———

FRANCIS

Jeep had one last remaining uncle, Olive and Judy's fifth brother, Francis. Everybody in the family adored him. He was retired from working as an anesthesiologist in England and sent Judy money every month that she sorely needed to augment her pension. Jeep said he would be able to tell me how Olive and the rest of the family came to be expelled. Judy thought he would know whether or not Olive had cooperated with the CIA.

"We are so many Yangs, I hope you can keep up," Francis said, laughing when he greeted me in the front garden of the semi-detached house he shared with his daughter in a suburb of London. He was tall for a

Figure 7.1. Francis Yang pictured with Louisa Benson on the Thai border in the 1960s.

Kokang man, with a shock of gray hair and square glasses. He looked like any normal retired doctor and not a former rebel leader.

When Olive was arrested and the revolution broke out, Francis was a university student with no formal military training. Francis was the bookish type who had never been interested in power, unlike Olive, and was suddenly called upon to lead guerilla troops alongside Jimmy and cousins in Kokang.

"There was one thing I could never do, and this is where I am different from my sister: I could never kill another man. And when I saw all the people around me killing each other, I didn't like that."

Francis said that's why he ultimately decided to surrender and become a doctor. To learn to do the opposite thing of killing people.

There was immense pressure as they prepared for a surprise invasion of Kokang, with their ancestors' graves in the balance. But when Francis set out with his regiment of Kokang freedom fighters, and they had their first confrontation with the enemies occupying their home, something wasn't right.

"All the people we were fighting, they were all just like us," Francis said, trying to explain why he made the shameful decision to surrender.

He was mild-mannered and slow-moving as we sat together in his living room drinking tea. His military tattoo peeked out of the sleeve of his sky blue cardigan as he reached for his cup.

"You know, there was nobody like Olive. Olive always got her way, she didn't care what other people thought or if they said she couldn't do something because she was a woman," he said, filled with admiration. "Olive is a real playboy. Any woman we did not dare to talk to, Olive will talk to. She's a better man than us."

Francis had responded to the tumultuous events by leaving and then settling into the most ordinary life possible in exile. Since emigrating in 1980, he had returned to visit Myanmar only once and never went back to Kokang—not even to pay respects to his ancestors. Francis said that he preferred British politeness and the way people mind their own business around London.

Like Judy, he suffered from diabetes and dementia. All the wars and imprisonments blended into one confusing, painful memory as Francis tried to excavate them. He sometimes forgot what he was saying in the middle of a sentence, scrambling it with another. He seemed ashamed by his failing memory, especially when he couldn't remember when he got married. Francis had been plagued by the shame he felt for letting down all of his ancestors by surrendering, when he decided to become a doctor, and it was still palpable from across the table.

"It was like a trauma, I suppose," Francis said, explaining why he so rarely allowed himself to think about the past. "Even so, one day I would like my grandson to know what this old man did when he was young."

Francis said the Yang family's expulsion from Kokang started with whispers and soon turned into a mutiny. Their downfall happened, like for all leaders of Kokang, through the betrayal of a trusted deputy. Olive's right-hand man, Lo Hsing Han, suddenly emerged from prison and had convinced enough men to follow him instead of the Yang brothers.[2]

By the time Olive came out of Insein Prison, the Yang family no longer had a claim to rule the land that belonged to their ancestors.

"We were all terrible to Olive when she came out of prison," Francis said, describing the way the family had blamed her for their demise, for trusting in Lo Hsing Han, and squandering all the family's money on women. Even though the Yangs were licensed producers and traders of opium, they had at times been erroneously labeled narcotics traffickers because of Olive.

Francis admitted he had heaped on, too: Olive had humiliated the family, dishonored their ancestors, and left them destitute. Then, their seventh brother, Kenneth, fell ill. Francis couldn't say what, exactly. The way Francis phrased it, he descended into a depression and was struck by madness.

"He couldn't handle the grief; he couldn't function. But we never talked about it at all," Francis said, struggling to find the phrase for a substance-induced psychosis that followed a prolonged heroin habit. After Jimmy checked him into the psychiatric hospital north of Rangoon, he never made it out of the institution alive.

"We always knew it would be this way," Francis lamented, cryptically. I asked Francis if he was talking about the family curse, and he cringed as soon as I mentioned it. "I don't believe in the curse," he said, reflexively, "but I suppose it came true."

"You know, Judy says Olive is the curse," I said.

"No, no," Francis laughed, and then shook his head. "That place, Kokang, there is nothing there after all these years of war. You know, opium is a crop just like any other, and it was all we have. There is nothing there for people, just opium; is that not a curse?"

Francis never directly intimated to me that he believed Kokang was cursed with opium, because he was too ashamed to admit of his own fraught relationship with the drug. He had learned to forgive his sister, once he had learned to forgive himself, for surviving the same madness that he said had afflicted his brother Kenneth.

From others in the family, I later learned the two brothers Francis and Kenneth had both turned to heroin in their time of tumult as rebels on the border. He and Kenneth both spiraled; Francis had lost years of his life to resorting to petty crimes to be able to feed his habit. Had it not been for his uncle, who arranged for him to be married, Francis would never have gotten clean. Kenneth, who had other complicating factors, fared less well, and Francis bore that guilt until today.

"Last time I spoke to Olive, I said I'm sorry on behalf of all my brothers and sisters. I'm so sorry for how we treated you. We were wrong."

Francis explained the only time he had returned home to visit Olive had been over a decade ago, apologizing for his behavior had been on the top of his list. Olive hadn't made a big fuss about accepting his apology at the time, but Francis could tell she was moved.

"I told her, from now on, you are my brother."

Francis said when he called Olive "brother," though there were no tears falling, he saw moisture forming in her eyes. Francis's voice trembled, plagued by his own regret, and as he cleared his throat, I felt a knot forming in my own.

"But you know it's too late now. The damage is already done. We have already hurt her so many times, all those years. Now it's too late."

When we made dinner together, it took him nearly half an hour to fry an egg, because he kept forgetting that he had already buttered the pan.

The following afternoon, he suggested we go eat fried chicken. "I know just the place. It's my favorite, and it's very nearby!"

But as we walked past the neatly manicured hedges towards the shops, he forgot where we were going and took me to the train station first by mistake instead, so it took us a while to find even though it was just around the corner.

"What sort of man would you like to marry?" he asked me over the bucket of chicken he'd ordered.

"I don't know," I said, caught completely off guard. "Someone who's smart and makes me laugh."

"I think I know just the man for you," he said, with a grin. "My son, he is in Mandalay, and he fits your requirements exactly. And he is unmarried! What do you think?"

Francis was a doting grandfather to his daughter's son; he walked him to school and helped him with his homework. But he was not an heir to the Yang name. Like all the other male Yangs of his generation, Francis's son had produced no heirs, and it was the one outcome of the family curse with which he had not yet made peace.

"Have you ever smoked Burmese opium?" Francis asked me, quietly. He was so reluctant to talk about opium, his voice lowered to a conspiratorial whisper whenever the subject came up, because it was such a shameful business.

When I shook my head, he flashed such a deeply sympathetic look of pity that it made me laugh. Clearly, I didn't know what I was missing.

"The fragrance is so pleasant," Francis drifted off as he conjured the scent from his memory, closing his eyes and sinking deeper into his chair. Francis had spoken to me about how they used to smoke opium after dinner, like a nightcap, or as pain medication when they lived in Kokang. "I miss the feeling."

"Did you ever personally guard an opium caravan?" I asked.

"Let me tell you this, Gabby, one time, we had a line of one hundred mules, it was so long it would have reached from here to Eltham station," he dramatically asked me to not take notes on this part.

Their mules passed through checkpoints without being bothered, and Francis was shocked that they had even managed to bribe the Burmese officials in the first place.

"We walked in such a large group across the border. It was really impossible to miss this line of mules. That's how we got the guns for our army," Francis said, explaining that it had been the same trading post where Olive had once traded opium for guns, too.

"Did Olive ever talk about trading opium with the CIA or working for them?" I asked.

"You know people love to talk, even I want to know how Olive always got away with everything," Francis said, explaining that Olive always seemed to find a way around the rules. "We just thought those weapons came from General Chennault's men. We didn't realize they were CIA until afterwards."

"After what?" I asked.

"After we were expelled," Francis said. "You know all this CIA, DEA, I used to think they were the good guys—they were just as corrupt as the rest of them. They were all working together. As soon as Jimmy needed them, they didn't want to know him."

"Francis, were you also cooperating with the CIA?" I asked, stunned. I had been so focused on Olive's history with the agency, I hadn't bothered to ask Francis about his.

"Not exactly cooperating . . ." Francis trailed off, lamenting the weird trick the agency had played on the family. "They sure did help out Lo Hsing Han, though."

"What do you mean?" I asked.

"I'll tell you about that another day," he said, then gestured to the ether, as if to say one could never be sure who was listening.

Before the end of my visit I explained to Francis what happened with the men in the hotel in Muse. "Duan didn't want to meet me," I admitted, sheepishly.

"I'm not surprised to hear that Duan did not want to talk to you. He will probably think you are working together with the CIA."

"Do you think Olive would talk to me?" I asked.

"I don't know, I think Olive would like you. And Olive likes to tell stories about heroes. I haven't thought about these things in years, you know, but I will remember more." Francis promised, before urging me to return soon.

Figure 7.2.   Francis Yang pictured in the backyard of his London home, 2015, holding a treasured portrait of himself with Louisa Benson.
GABRIELLE PALUCH.

CHAPTER EIGHT

In Prison, in Love, in Mandalay

IN ONE WIDESPREAD FAIRYTALE, OLIVE WAS FOREVER INDEBTED TO LO HSING Han for saving her life.

Down on his luck and drowning in gambling debts, a young Lo first fell in love with Olive while crouched by the side of a busy trade route, intending to shake down a few merchants until he had enough money to show his face again at the mahjong parlor.

At first, when Olive came galloping down the road, he thought it was a man. But as soon as Lo spooked the horse and drew his weapon, he realized his folly. Lo was momentarily frozen, stunned by her unafraid smile and glistening teeth.

Olive smacked the weapon from a stunned Lo's hands with a bullwhip, and instantly had him subdued on the ground, with a pistol pressed to his face.

"I am Miss Yang Number Two, and who are you?" Olive said.

"I did not know I was in the presence of nobility. Have mercy on me!" Lo pleaded, once he realized who Olive was, swearing undying fealty, in exchange for his life.

Much to Lo's surprise, when Olive then took him to the family court to see Edward. Instead of being punished, Olive paid his gambling debts and he was recruited into his personal force of bodyguards to earn a meager salary. Lo stopped spending so much time at the mahjong parlor, and became a good soldier. He quickly gained the trust of the ruling family.

When Olive was made commander of a Secret Army battalion the night before they were to set out into battle, Lo was suddenly moved by harbored unspoken romantic feelings for Olive to dissuade her from going.

"You'll risk certain death, master. I cannot be there to save you," Lo said.

"I would risk shame!" Olive replied, unyieldingly.

Olive set off on horseback with four hundred men, riding into the night to battle the wretched Burmese, who slaughtered them within three days.

Lo, distraught by the news, had already started mourning Olive's death when a courier arrived to inform him Olive was taken hostage within the first few hours of battle. Knowing the cruelty of the Burmese prison guards, Lo lost no time.

Lo packed saddled up the fastest horse in the family's stable, and rode in disguise behind enemy lines, directly to the prison where Olive was being held. With sacks of gold bars from the family court, Lo bribed a prison guard who handed him a key.

Lo returned at midnight to open Olive's cell. He fell to his knees and knelt at her feet, Lo confessed he was driven by guilt and passionate love to rescue her. The two then silently scurried out of the prison, and saddled up, galloping with gunfire at their backs all the way back to Kokang. Upon their safe return, Olive, suddenly taken by the heroic gesture, agreed to marry Lo in front of her assembled family.

But after years of wedded opium-trafficking bliss, Lo was blinded by his own ambition, and was swayed by Burmese authorities to betray Olive and her brothers. In exchange for delivering them to the Burmese, he would receive his own opium empire on their land.

While swearing his undying love for Olive, Lo took it upon himself to tie her in restraints, as the Burmese troops approached their home. During the struggle, Olive kicked and screamed, and reached for the guns in her bedside table, but she was too slow. Olive had supposedly become too satisfied and docile to maintain her sharpshooting skill. Her last words to him, as he bound her up, were to call him a dog.[1]

* * *

Up in Kokang, Olive insisted on the traditional pomp and circumstance of the ancestors' retinues, while wearing an American pilot's jacket. Whenever Olive showed up somewhere acting like the chieftain, Lo Hsing Han stood by to help her dismount. Then he would wordlessly present a tin of cigarettes and a light, so Olive could smoke as they proceeded with their business.[2]

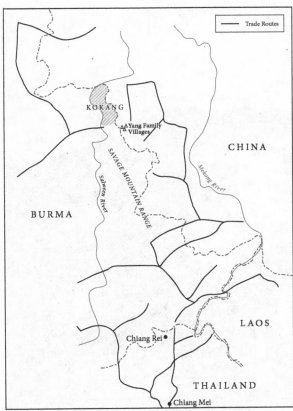

Map 8.1. A rough sketch of Olive's trade routes

Lo Hsing Han's father was a ranking officer who participated in the invasions and brought his son along wherever he went. The way Judy described it, Lo ingratiated himself to Olive in a way that made all the siblings uncomfortable.

At the Hke Hpok village, people knew Lo and Fat Huang were supposed to be Edward's men, but it was clear they were not carrying out the chieftain's errands. So they just started to call them Olive's Boys and went along with orders, because they were all slightly afraid.

Opium has been harvested in the same painstaking way for centuries until today. Just one acre of the fussy flowers could keep an entire family occupied day and night. After blossoming, the vibrantly shaded petals last just a few days before falling away from their pod. The pods produce a white sap when scored, which left to drain and dry in the afternoon sun, turns to a brown latex overnight that farmers collect in a sticky lump in the morning before dawn.

The farmers, who relied on their opium harvest for food, were concerned the rains had been a little thin that year. But with the newly arrived guerillas tending the fields, it was the biggest opium harvest Olive had

Figure 8.1.   Edward pictured with his generals ca. 1956.
YANG FAMILY PRIVATE COLLECTION.

ever seen. No hillside was left unplanted, including the recently abandoned fields of farmers who were frightened away.

"Land taxes! On the chieftain's sister's orders!"[3] Fat Huang would call out, when he went around to farmers' homes, demanding their opium, or rice if they had none. From wealthier households, Fat Huang helped himself to their cattle and mules, claiming they were needed for military purposes.

Mothers warned their children not to cross Fat Huang, because of the falling hole with the fire ants and pythons.

Figure 8.2.   Olive at the steps near the Guanyin Temple in Kokang ca. 1956.
YANG FAMILY PRIVATE COLLECTION.

One villager, however, noticed Fat Huang had gotten greedy; he had more mules than he cared to keep and started hawking them at the market in the next biggest town down the road on Savage Mountain.[4] The villager went to report Fat Huang to the police for robbery but found Lo Hsing Han's father as Edward's guard in Kokang administrative offices.

To voice his grievances, he went to see his village headman[5] with four fresh chicken eggs in a bowl, as was customary for filing a legal complaint. When his eggs mysteriously disappeared without a resolution, he brought four more. Ordinarily, if a village headman settled a complaint, the parties were invited to his home and required to get one another drunk before leaving the room. No resolution could be reached before drinking, nor after getting drunk, leaving a small window of time for discussion. If no resolution was reached, they could appeal to the chieftain. But nobody had been getting drunk with Fat Huang. And since Edward had moved to Lashio, nobody had been hearing appeals.

So the villager went across the ferry to ask the assistant resident what to do if they were being robbed and had no way to report the crimes.

"The men who are harassing us have free reign, because the chieftain's men are failing to enforce the law," the villager explained, exasperated.

"Rest assured, I will enquire with the Kokang State levies office myself," the assistant resident said.

Within a week, the assistant resident was convinced: in Edward's absence, his fearsome sister—who was neither man, nor woman—had claimed control of the entire state by sheer terror. He believed Olive had designs on Edward's seat of power, frightening people and harassing the border with stolen cattle and bandits.

"There is no womanly thing about her at all," the assistant resident told Sao Hom Hpa, alarmed by what he had learned about her robbing and looting her way into commanding an army. "She dresses like a man, acts like a bully, and administratively speaking is parallel with the *sawbwa* himself, and Edward's subordinates are too afraid to report it."

Sao Hom Hpa was hardly surprised to hear the news. Edward had been increasingly aloof and repeated reports to his office had gone unanswered.[6]

"Edward must be unaware of the depth of his sister's machinations. Since moving to Lashio, perhaps he doesn't know what is going on," the assistant resident said, hoping someone could talk some sense into Edward.

"Frankly speaking, I think Olive and Edward are in cahoots," Sao Hom Hpa speculated.

Finally, Sao Hom Hpa summoned Edward to Lashio to answer for his sister's misdeeds. Villagers were being robbed; eggs were disappearing. All the misbehaving levies were under her command. Olive had been using Edward's officers for her own errands, collecting taxes without permission. Some villagers even claimed their sons were being forced into joining the army, for secret missions along the border with China. The headmen, they claimed amnesia.

Sao Hom Hpa accused Edward of allowing Olive and her bandits to roam at will preying on villagers and had done little to remove the Chinese infiltration in his garrisons.

"Olive has nothing to do with these people," Edward insisted, insulted by the scathing report. Kokang was very much under the control of his brothers and cousins, Edward didn't believe any of it. "I have been reliably informed by my deputies."

"Are you certain?" Sao Hom Hpa asked. Surely Edward could not be so naive as to believe his sister's denials, and Sao Hom Hpa knew better than to underestimate Olive.

"The assistant resident, from his safety perch across the river, has never been to Kokang and could hardly truly know the situation better than they do," Edward reassured Sao Hom Hpa.

Over one week that same month, three hundred men set off with their first big Secret Army opium shipment set off with General Li. All their export papers required the stamp of the official Yang family copper seal. They had assembled 463 mules in five armed caravans along the arduous route to the Secret Army base in Mong Hsat, which took nearly a month.[7]

The Kokang opium General Li brought to the trading post for Olive was of such reputable quality, it fetched higher prices from the traders who took it across to Thailand. The porters who hiked opium down in Chiang Mai handed it off to Mr. Ho's security detail.

Down at SEA Supply in Bangkok, a former Flying Tigers man named Dutch Brongersma would receive telegrammed instructions. He would show up at the airfield in Bangkok to help load his Dakota with weapons and equipment to fly north to Burma to the Secret Army. On his return, Dutch refueled in Chiang Mai, where a special Thai police force helped him load opium from Mr. Ho's warehouse onto his plane. Dutch logged over one hundred flights shuttling weapons and opium along the Burma route since the failed invasions. He was a bit of a man about town, and he must have gotten drunk or been otherwise indiscreet with a journalist, because before long someone had described his route in a newspaper.[8]

The Secret Army received Dutch's drops at their base and trading post in Mong Hsat, which by then had an all-weather runway and military academy. Though very much in Burma, it was called the Anti-Communist Anti-Soviet University of Yunnan Province. Chinese-speakers from around the state came to attend training with tactical instructors who were flown in. All sorts of specialists and American goods arrived, even mechanics and jeeps. After graduating as trained guerillas, cadres were assigned to teams throughout the region.[9]

"The invasion has failed because the people are insufficiently prepared for liberation," the Borderland Poet declared at their base in Kokang, now the headquarters of their anti-communist third force. He had ambitious strategic plans for their column. "Small guerilla operations for sabotage attacks behind enemy lines in Red China would be much more effective."

As a base for these attacks, on their maps, spanning from the border in the north with Tibet, all the way south to the Bay of Bengal, they would establish a multi-ethnic Chinese-speaking anti-communist state in Burma; connected by a massive smuggling route spanning the entire length of the Salween River. Thanks to Chennault's men, they had the weapons to be able to execute it. Olive was on board with the Borderland Poet's plans. Duan's village was included in the territory they intended to take, as was Sao Hom Hpa's native town.[10]

An enemy Chinese communist regiment had set up camp in a small town across the river at the border crossing at the Wanting Bridge, which was the busiest trading post in Sao Hom Hpa's land. That was where Duan's family operated a fleet of trucks. The border with Red China was closed to everybody except merchants like them.[11]

The caravan trade was booming because of widespread shortages, and all the communist troops' necessities like medicine, cotton for uniforms, ammunition, or watches were coming from Burma. Especially rationed strategic goods like petroleum or tires had to be illegally smuggled.[12]

Olive's bravado was astonishing while carrying out work for the Secret Army, disguised as a caravan trader.[13, 14]

"It's been a long journey," Olive would declare loudly to the guards at the border crossing, before asking their names, and whether they liked their whiskey. "You don't mind if we break for lunch, do you?"

When Olive arrived at the border together with her wares, she would linger in the station, running her hands through the sacks of rice that concealed illicit goods or special sabotaged supplies to be delivered to the communists. Defective batteries, slow watches, or bars of soap containing itching powder were mixed in with usual contraband.

Across the bridge in the enemy Chinese towns, blaring loudspeakers reminded people to "defeat the American imperialists!" They broadcast Chinese opera and communist slogans all day long and could not be turned off.

Olive posed as a double-agent, concealing false information in wax-sealed messages within her goods, before returning to Kokang with details about their troops and bases.[15]

When the communist regiment across the border bought foodstuff like pea flour, they cut it with laxatives so they would be at the mercy of their bowels. Then, the communists came back to barter for a whole truck full of penicillin.[16]

Nearly everybody at the trading post was gathering intelligence. Monks, women—even children were recruited into a children's intelligence corps. They trained to hide secret messages in their clothes. When they sometimes darted across the border while chasing crickets or an errant ball, officials never paid them any mind.[17]

When Burmese officials forbade trucks or petroleum to be traded to China, the Secret Army units from Kokang set their sights on taking control of all the roads to China. They ambushed merchants, threatening, extorting them for half their goods in the name of the Secret Army on the way from Mandalay to the border. They even killed other smugglers.[18]

Olive's family had cornered the market on the illegal auto trade, so when an enemy communist official willing to trade opium for a Jeep came to Old Street Village, Olive ordered men to disassemble and ferry it across the river in pieces. Then it was smuggled across the border to the official, who became the proud owner of the third motor vehicle in his whole county.[19]

Other officials at the biggest trading post in Sao Hom Hpa's land eventually had to be withdrawn, and any violence on those roads was said to have been carried out in Olive's name. For a time, any man who dared travel their way with a truck full of goods owed a fee for the privilege of staying alive: one-fifth of their cargo's value in tolls, payable at the excise tax office located in Olive's operation area. The assistant resident for Kokang, who had never actually made it past the southern border, requested to be withdrawn too.[20]

"Guerilla warfare is economic warfare!" The Borderland Poet was fond of saying.

They expanded their trade routes north all the way to the rugged Himalayan foothills of Burma's Kachin State just on the border with Tibet. The Borderland Poet went to establish a base—when the wind was high, the moon was bright, and tigers roared in the night—on a Kachin chieftain's land, known for mining the finest of jade. His borders with China, too, were disputed.

"The Burmese borderlands are the ancestral home of all living beings belonging to China," the Borderland Poet said, noting the barbarians there wore similar clothes to his compatriots in Yunnan and spoke his same native dialect.[21]

Fat Huang robbed the route south of Kokang to Savage Mountain, torturing merchants he robbed with unusual cruelty, even after they surrendered their goods. The Burmese official assigned to the trading post there was an odious relative of Sao Hom Hpa. He demanded even higher bribes than usual, such that villagers who needed to buy rice couldn't afford to cross the border. He was ambushed by a group of angry Wa villagers who beheaded him.[22] A great number of people had reasons to celebrate his absence when he was murdered and suspected Fat Huang of plotting his death.

Not long thereafter, Olive set off with a Yang family delegation of Kokang muleteers to establish villages on a few acres of unfarmable Wa wasteland on Savage Mountain.[23] They told the chieftain they were there to protect him from the communist infiltration, and in exchange for paying taxes, they were allowed to set up a little string of villages with a trade outpost and caravan route.[24]

The Secret Army commander in charge of operations in the new Yang family villages was also a prospector, who knew the mountains in that area well.[25] Because there was no land to farm, all the families could do was mine or trade. It was strategically placed, right where it could interfere with the communists' plans.

Figure 8.3.   A market in a multi-ethnic village, Bangyang, which eventually became a unity village. INSTITUTE OF HISTORY AND LINGUISTICS, ACADEMIA SINICA.

As more people poured in to work in the villages, they started working parts of the mine that had tin or lead. Judy never saw for herself, but she said with the prospector's help, they very soon hit on a veritable treasure of silver and gold.[26]

By the time the 1952 opium harvest began arriving in Chiang Mai, Harold had moved into a villa on the outskirts of Chiang Mai with the intention of turning it into a zoo that would serve as cover for clandestine intelligence activity. The happenings of Olive's trade routes were making their way into classified reports Harold translated for the new CIA station chief.[27]

Some of the opium Olive sent to Thailand with General Li that year came from the communists in China, revealing their troop positions, road construction, and valuable insights from behind the bamboo curtain.[28] Harold received more concerning news about communists misbehaving in Wa villages, too.

In one instance, approaching Chinese communist troops were so frightened by the Wa villagers who gathered a welcome party, that they started firing, and killed thirty people, including women and children.

Wa escapees flowed into the little Baptist church where the Secret Army commander set up a radio post with SEA Supply's help during the invasion. Among them, the first to receive the gospel from Harold's father. The retaliation had been particularly brutal around Harold's old mission in Yunnan, where his first converts were such firm believers, they refused to be turned communist. They had been told by their communist officials they could no longer be Baptists. Their homes were burned, believers were snatched away for reeducation. One had even returned to say he'd been intimidated by being taken to see the mass execution of three hundred reactionaries, a display that would likely have left him unimpressed. Some had been hiding in a cave for months before leaving.[29]

A large regiment of troops moved in and all the great religious leaders fled, taking with them the knowledge of their cultural practices. Then the communists declared their town a unity village, and it became a model commune.

"The Wa have a special feeling of affection and respect for white men and are unanimous in their desire to have the white man assist them and even rule them."[30] Harold was desperate to help them. Harold knew the Wa were capable warriors. He felt a sense of guardianship for the people who had put so much faith in him, as to give him their magical staff.

Harold also knew the Wa are prone to tribal disputes, especially when it comes to outsiders looting their precious minerals. He may have simply believed he was doing the right thing.

Figure 8.4. Wa chieftain of Gengma, Han Futing, whose seized letter about the weapons drops got Olive jailed. ACADEMIA SINICA.

"The Wa rulers are particularly anxious for American assistance and offer to disclose ore deposits," Harold wrote. "They could present an effective barrier to communist encroachments if given capable American leadership and proper aid."

Before long, Harold was sending spies behind enemy lines, who operated along a network of joint CIA–Secret Army radio intelligence outposts next to mining operations around Savage Mountain.[31]

All around Sao Hom Hpa's land, the Secret Army men from Olive'sgarrisons started to infiltrate. The ruler of Mongshu paid tithes to Sao Hom Hpa on his ruby mine and was a second-born son, whose older brother felt scorned because he had been passed over by their father as successor. After being visited by a Secret Army agent from their base in Kokang, his younger brother chieftain was carried away by an angry mob. He declared himself ruler, conscripted their men into a Secret Army regiment underneath him, and they started panning for gems.[32]

Olive's erstwhile husband, too, had spent the better part of the last year proving himself an effective commander battling rebels, Kachin and otherwise. He earned accolades from his chieftain brother, and was made village headman upon his return.[33] Duan had perhaps been expecting to find his firstborn son at home, but he was not there. When Duan sent word for Olive asking to see his progeny, he was refused. There was no response from the Yang family court.

Instead, Duan found while he'd been away, Olive's men had been there, asking around if there was anybody who might be thinking of joining the resistance. A number of people in his village and even his

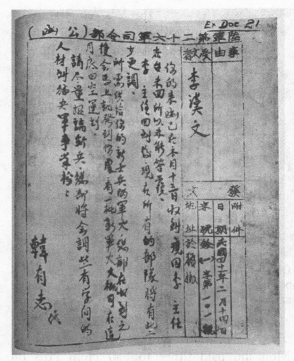

Figure 8.5. The letter chieftain Han Futing sent confirming the CIA weapons drops to Li Wenhuan (General Li) which Olive helped retrieve in 1951, one of the pieces of evidence that got Olive jailed. INFORMATION MINISTRY OF BURMA

brother had decided they would.[34] Duan informed Sao Hom Hpa of the infiltration in his villages, but the Burma Army was too tied up elsewhere to help.

Sometime in October 1952, Olive was riding in a jeep to a trading post only to find the usual border guard was not there. Chinese county officials had closed the border, and she was detained by the sentry. Olive realized she was in deep trouble when she was transferred to a higher-security prison in Mandalay, on suspicion of colluding with insurgents. Specifically, General Li and the Wa chieftain, who had registered their arms at the 101 garrison. The Burma Army had captured a letter they signed, confirming the receipt of the weapons dropped to them by the Americans.[35]

Sao Hom Hpa had pleaded for a state of emergency. All foreigners were forbidden from entering the country, and unlicensed travel of any kind in Shan State was made illegal. Sao Hom Hpa summoned Duan and his other vassal chieftains to take matters into their own hands with a few leftover rifles from World War II and homemade guns.[36]

General Ne Win sent a regiment to help liberate Sao Hom Hpa's villages. The Ponytailed Bandit sabotaged them, burning down four

Figure 8.6.   Edward inspects troops after Operation Maha against the Kuomintang troops in Kokang. INFORMATION MINISTRY OF BURMA.

barracks of the Burma Army headquarters near Lashio, then started burning swaths of Kachin villages on his way back across the Salween.[37]

Duan and his men battled the Ponytailed Bandit all the way to a very remote village where they unleashed unimaginable terror. Duan was forced to hide in the headman's widow's home as the Ponytailed Bandit and his men started raping, killing, and looting all the villagers' food stores before torching their homes. The wife of one of the the Kachin chieftains was so violently raped, she was still suffering grievous injuries weeks later.[38] Duan's men finally prevailed after a dramatic six-hour battle that left ten dead in pools of blood in the middle of the village. But the Ponytailed Bandit was still at large in Kokang.[39]

General Ne Win asked Edward to help lead a secret assault to arrest the fugitives and drive the Secret Army from their stronghold in his own state. But all his levies were loyal to Olive, so as the Burma Army regiment approached Kokang for their joint-operation, Lo Hsing Han and the Kokang Self-Defense Force helped light a strategic fire all along the eastern bank of the Salween River.[40]

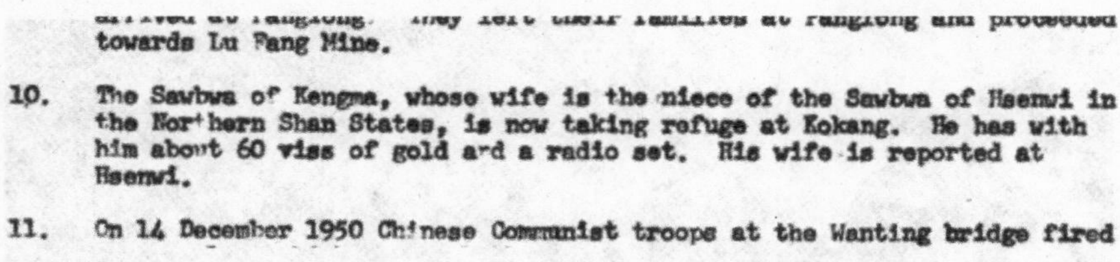

towards Lu Fang Mine.

10.   The Sawbwa of Kengma, whose wife is the niece of the Sawbwa of Hsenwi in
      the Northern Shan States, is now taking refuge at Kokang. He has with
      him about 60 viss of gold and a radio set. His wife is reported at
      Hsenwi.

11.   On 14 December 1950 Chinese Communist troops at the Wanting bridge fired

Figure 8.7.   CIA document describing chieftain of Gengma Han Futing's where-abouts in late 1950.

While the flames kept the Burmese troops at bay, Fat Huang concealed their materials, burying weapons from the 101 garrison in caves. Edward swept through Kokang with his levies, with orders to shoot on sight any man with unregistered arms. Nearly one thousand Secret Army men under General Li escaped east, protected by the fire.[41] They fled south toward Savage Mountain where they encountered Chinese communist attackers along the way, until they eventually had to swim east across the Mekong river, where they were marooned in Laos.

Fat Huang knew acts of treason carried the penalty of death. They say to prove fealty to Edward, Fat Huang personally went to execute the Ponytailed Bandit—but even he escaped.[42]

Edward was congratulated for completing his mission and sent his two thousand men away with all of their mules to help the Burmese elite battalions eliminate the Secret Army's university and airstrip further south.[43]

The magnitude of global events Olive's actions had set in motion became clear while she was in prison. In March 1953, Jimmy and Edward helped introduce a report to parliament about the Secret Army incursion, including all the details the army had gathered about Olive.

As the Burma Army liberated villages that had been occupied by Olive's collaborators, they found evidence of heinous crimes. The Burmese commander who had driven them from their strongholds and found their American weapons, also found the bodies of their German small-weapons instructors from the French legion from their university and an American, who died in the fray.[44] In investigators' reports, Olive's name appeared repeatedly. Olive had been seen receiving American

Dakota airdrops with the Ponytailed Bandit, who had raped, looted, and murdered his way across the Salween.

The same report was soon introduced to the United Nations Security Council. Though Olive was one of many, she was the only Union of Burma citizen singled out by name as a recipient of US arms for the purposes of launching an attack on Chinese soil. By April 23, the U.N. adopted a resolution that condemned foreign forces in Burma, forcing the United States to fly the Secret Army out on General Chennault's planes.[45] Olive had been unanimously condemned by every nation in the world.

With Olive in prison and the fighting in his village subsiding, Duan took the opportunity to come inspect his progeny for the first time at Edward's house in Lashio. Jeep was almost certainly too young to remember this day but swears he recalls vividly how excited he was to meet his father. Jeep was expecting to be taken home, so he was heartbroken when his father entered the house and barely cast a glance his way. They exchanged no words directly. Duan explained to Edward he had plans to remarry, then he left without Jeep. Ordinarily, divorces were settled with either blood or silver—but Duan was happy to leave empty-handed. It was the closest encounter father and son would ever have. Back in his village, Duan took two more concubines and immediately got to work making new heirs.

"Your mother has forbidden your father from speaking to you," Edward told Jeep, when he asked why he had been left behind.

Judy, who had to move away from Kokang to escape the violence that followed the Secret Army's banditry, was disgusted to see that Olive didn't show more remorse for the suffering she had caused. While Olive was away there had been raids by armed members of the Chinese Communist

1. The Chinese Communists, commanded by WAI Kung are purchasing raw cotton for kyats 570 per 100 viss at Ma-Li-Pei.[2] YANG Chin Hsiu has supplied them with 7,000 viss of cotton. The LEE Chang Company has sent the Communists 12,000 viss of cotton and 300 Roman trade mark waterproof watches. WAI Kung's officers at Muse (97-54; 24-00) have sent out tribesmen to buy 400 additional watches.

Figure 8.8. CIA document from December 1952 describing deals with communist trading partners by YANG Chin Hsiu (Olive). These were likely the last trades at the border before Olive was arrested.

Party, infiltrating Kokang, looking to put Olive on trial as a counterrevolutionary, perhaps even kill her.[46]

Judy laughed when she heard the romantic prison-break story about young Lo Hsing Han and Olive, because even if Lo had broken her out, Olive wouldn't have wanted to leave.

"Olive was in heaven in Mandalay prison," Judy said, without much sympathy for her sister.

Olive was cut off from the upheaval of the outside world, in a jail yard full of long-haired beauties, without a man in sight. Judy said Olive seduced the most powerful woman in the building, to make her stay more comfortable.

The siblings reunited Jeep with his mother when she was released a year and a half later. They took him to Olive's new two-story house in Mandalay, not far from the prison. Suddenly, Jeep was in what he described as a very weird living arrangement together with his mother's prison warden, Daw Htay Htay.

At first, Jeep said he was under the false impression he, too, had gone to live in prison together with Olive, because they were living with Daw Htay Htay. Later, when he was older, Jeep wondered if Olive hadn't bribed Daw Htay Htay with the house, in order to get out of prison, because they were constantly fighting.

Judy said warden Daw Htay Htaw was a fat, plain-looking Burmese woman who was partially blind and completely infatuated. She was the first woman who truly loved Olive, and they experienced something of a sexual awakening together.

Best to let Judy tell you herself.

CHAPTER NINE

YOU SHALL NOT SAY HER NAME

ONE DAY, I ASKED JUDY IF SHE THOUGHT OLIVE WAS A MAN.

"Olive dresses like a man, wants to be treated like a man, wants to get girls like a man, but Olive is a woman who can do anything like a man. That's why she has the artificial penis," Judy concluded.

I looked at her quizzically, unsure if I had heard her correctly.

Judy assumed a conspiratorial stance, which she often did when she was about to say something crass or straightforward.

"You know what they say, I have never seen it, but I have heard, Olive had an artificial penis on a belt."

She gestured toward her waist as she said this, catching me off guard, and I began to laugh.

"Don't laugh, Gabby! That's how they make sex. Do you think it's true? Can they have such a thing?"

I composed myself and assured Judy such a thing existed.

"Where?" she asked.

"You can find anything on the internet," I suggested.

"Oh." Judy sat back in her chair, satisfied with that answer. "I heard she got it in Mandalay, when she was in prison."

The object Judy described, as she had been told, was a custom-made lover's gift from warden Daw Htay Htay, who had apparently smuggled it in at Olive's request. It was made of teak and had a leather holster that attached itself to a belt in the same way a gun holster would.

119

"Daw Htay Htay really loved Olive," Judy concluded, wistfully, "now she's dead and gone."

"Are any of Olive's girlfriends still alive?" I asked.

"Wah Wah Win Shwe should know more about Olive's special belt, and she is still living in her house, too. Why don't you ask her about it?" Judy suggested, matter-of-factly. "Ask her about how she got the house."

WAH WAH

Soon, I managed to arrange an audience with Wah Wah at the property where she had once lived with Olive.

As I walked toward the compound, I passed the building at the address that had once been Jimmy's house. It was now occupied by an elegant shop house for gems owned by Lo Hsing Han's family. I could see why Judy never went to that street anymore. It was full of monuments to their family's lost fortune.

The house where Olive had once lived with Wah Wah had been a modest but spacious home with an exceptionally large garden down the street, that Olive had occasionally used as a safehouse for the goods her trading businesses smuggled at the border. Now, all I could see was a hulking wedding cake of a house with columns and several expensive cars in a paved motorpark. Judy told me that some years ago, Wah Wah had demolished Olive's house, subdivided the property, and resold the back half of the lot.

Making sure nobody could see me, I went to investigate the property behind Wah Wah's house, which was now a partially abandoned hotel and nightclub. It looked like it had been so long since an actual guest had stayed there, that they didn't bother to turn on the lights in the lobby.

The property's essential function had never changed. It was sold to a corporation belonging to the Wa tribesmen who had once fought alongside Olive. As I walked through the darkened halls into a garden, I remembered the story I'd heard about a whiskey-soaked revenge-beheading to have taken place there. I could understand now why Wah Wah's walls were so high.

Fiure 9.1. Wah Wah Win Shwe holding a photo of herself at age sixteen, performing a traditional Burmese dance.

GABRIELLE PALUCH.

Wah Wah rarely acted these days, and films were not as glamorous as they once were in Myanmar, but she was still such a big celebrity that I was greeted by a publicist. Wah Wah wore her signature large-frame sunglasses indoors, dripping in pearls and rubies, draped in golden silk threads. On the wall behind her was a life-size portrait of her from her most iconic role in the film which launched her into fame.

Her family milled around the room, drifting in to check in on us periodically, and a maid brought us tea, as she began to recite her origin story.

"I came into the film world in 1961 when a classmate introduced me to a producer. I had been registered to study medicine at Rangoon University, but I didn't want to be a doctor, I wanted to be an actress. My first film was a surprise hit. That's why I say: I was born to be a star."

Wah Wah pointing to her three Myanmar Academy Awards, golden statuettes displayed nearby and plucked the one with a bent star off the shelf. "I won those decades ago, back when it was harder to win, the awards really meant something. That was my first one, even General Ne Win was pleased with my performance." She said, referring to the dictator who finally removed Olive's family from power, and handed it to me.

"When did you first fall in love?" I asked.

"I met my husband and have been in love ever since, and my husband is the only man I ever dated." Wah Wah said, as if to emphasize that she had been a virgin on her wedding day. Her husband, a beloved actor and director, was upstairs in bed because he had recently lost a leg to gangrene, so he could not join.

I had been hoping to learn more about what it was like to be wooed by Olive. But Judy's suggestion that I ask about Olive's special belt was undoubtedly ill-advised, given that Wah Wah took great pride in her reputation.

Wah Wah's ruby ring glinted in the light as she put her teacup to her lips.

"That one was very expensive," she said, noticing my gaze had fixated on it.

"Where did you get it?" I asked, hoping she'd say Olive had given it to her.

"Oh, no, no—I have many, many jewels. I can't even keep track of where they all came from," she replied.

When her publicist drifted away and I finally felt bold enough to ask her if she'd had a secret lesbian relationship she was now trying to hide from her family.

"One more thing, do you know Olive Yang?" I asked. Wah Wah stepped back a bit, and her expression fell. She indicated I should gather my things without speaking, and then started showing me out, pretending not to hear. So I waited until we were just at the door to ask again.

"I heard that before, you had a wife," I whispered.

"Who told you that?" she whispered, angrily.

"I read it," I said, then added for authority, "in a book."

Once Wah Wah had recomposed herself, she resumed her prior confidence, stroking the pearls around her neck. "You know some people are just jealous, they want to say horrible things about people."

"Why would they say that?" I asked.

"They say I'm a lesbian, because in the entertainment industry you know there are many people like that, who are man and woman both."

"Is Olive both a man and a woman?" I asked.

"I don't know who you're talking about with that name. You shall not say her name," Wah Wah said.

"But I heard that this house was once hers," I said, as she shooed me out the door. "The Kokang ruler's sister?"

"That's nonsense. I inherited it! Some people just want to spread horrible lies. Who told you this?" she demanded and indicated I should put on my shoes. "You must have heard more, you must have heard more. Who sent you?"

"Nobody, I just wanted to know if it's true."

I began to apologize, but she had already closed the door.

Judy was already waiting for me in her chair in the sitting room when I greeted her through the gate the next day. She was always far more eager for me to meet people who resented Olive, thrilled to hear about my failed visit.

"You see? It's true! Now you can see why nobody wants to talk about Olive. Nobody," she said, laughing, as I sat down in my usual spot, recounting the tense exchange we had at the door. "You are lucky Wah Wah Win Shwe didn't slap your face!"

When I told her Wah Wah claimed she'd inherited the house, Judy grew indignant.

"That is how Wah Wah stole it, she convinced her to give it to her, legally!"

When Olive emerged from Insein Prison, destitute and stricken, Wah Wah wouldn't let her back in her own house. All the siblings knew what was going on. Wah Wah had been with men while Olive was in prison. At first Olive didn't want to believe it, because Wah Wah had been leading her on.

But as soon as Olive heard that Wah Wah had married a man, Olive hired an infamously showy lawyer to get her house back. Wah Wah returned from her honeymoon, only to find she had been sued. At first, it seemed like the lawsuit was going well; the tabloids reported dramatic testimony about their love affairs, humiliating Wah Wah. The lawyer even convinced Olive to sue her jailer Daw Htay Htay, for their shared house in Mandalay, too. But ultimately, Olive lost both her houses.

"You see Wah Wah doesn't really love Olive, she is with a man now, in her house. It is always like that for Olive. Me, I don't want to be loved by anybody, I'm happy here on my own. She is unlucky in love," Judy said. She rarely showed sympathy for Olive before, and it was touching to see her take her side.

"That's when Lo Hsing Han told everything to the court, then she went to prison again," Judy said, and her face soured.

"Always in and out and in and out of prison. I feel bad for my sister, when people are successful because of her and don't want to know her when she's down," Judy concluded, shaking her head.

"If Olive was so famous for marrying Wah Wah, why were there so many people who didn't know she was gay?" I asked Judy.

"Because they wrote it in a book, a rubbish book," Judy said, spitting her words. "A British man who fell in love with Olive wrote it. All full of this disgusting sex stuff."

CHAPTER TEN

Sensuous Opium Queen, Miss Hairy Legs

In OPIUM VENTURE, OLIVE *WAS THE INFAMOUS SAVAGE AND SENSUOUS OPIUM queen, who had seduced the lucky British fellow in exchange for favors from the courts.*

Judge Gerald Sparrow said he had just arrived to serve on the court in northern Thailand, because his predecessor had met a mysterious, untimely death. His clerks believed it was a murder ordered by an infamous banished Princess living across the border in Burma. The court had imprisoned one of her agents.

The Princess was said to have almost single-handedly driven the sudden unprecedented amount of drugs coming out of Burma, amassing unthinkable wealth in a splendid palace. She was said to be a slave to the drug. Opium was her husband, her lover, her god.

Having gained control of every single opium trade route from Laos, she commanded her army of five hundred spies to do the dirty business of her criminal cartel with abominable cruelty. The Princess kept her men as slaves, and paid them in opium so they would be bound to her by their addictions. She tortured her men by extinguishing Burmese cigars on the palms of their hands, and stuck them with burning hot needles she kept in her purse.

Sparrow received a mysterious written invitation to her palace, and decided to accept, because he heard she was young, unmarried, and beautiful to look at. He told his superiors he was on a mission to investigate the murderous mastermind of a criminal opium empire, and set out to meet her.

During his time with the Princess, Sparrow was wined, dined, and massaged into an opium-laced stupor at the palace. But it did not blind him to her evil ways.

She whipped and caged her employees like cattle when they didn't carry out her tasks. On Sparrow's second night, when a thief was discovered in their midst, the Princess requested he be brought to her chamber in the evening to be punished. The servants asked if she would like him to be delivered pre-beaten.

The Princess derived power and sexual excitement from the terror in the eyes of those she punished. With an army at her disposal, she had begun to torture malefactors every month; when there were none to beat, she sought out excuses to satisfy her unnatural sexual craving. Among her slaves was a blue-eyed American, who spoke perfect Shan, and could not say from whence he came. They all seemed entranced by her, as if under some sort of spell.

Sparrow was lent a beautiful steed for an all-day ride through thickly forested trails. As night fell, they approached a hillside field of spectacular blooming red poppies, with a striking circle of white ones glowing in the moonlight in their midst.

The Princess explained they were a rare albino species known as midnight poppies, and to have glimpsed them is a privilege. Sparrow, though mesmerized by the haunting beauty of the blossoms, realized he was in too deep.

The Princess spotted a leopard in the jungle brush, and shot it through the eye, killing it with a single bullet. Then, inspired by the thrill of the hunt, she cunningly seduced a reluctant Sparrow with urgent passion. Sparrow remarked she retained a freshness that seemed to say she seldom had a man.

"Not a bad day. The leopard, and you," the flushed Princess murmured after the deed.

Finally, the Princess offered Sparrow an enticing contract. In exchange for becoming her vast opium empire's exclusive agent, she would pay him an unimaginable sum of money. However, only under the condition that he marry her, and remain in Burma as her prisoner.

The next morning while eating breakfast, one of the Princess's disgruntled agents shot her in the back. The amassed servants and soldiers suddenly begged Sparrow to stay and rule them as their king. They desperately needed a leader, and had reverence for the white man.

But the Princess survived the shooting with Sparrow's attentive medical care, and he decided he could not stay in such a depraved world. Sparrow lamented he would never experience the rapture he had with such a fierce, untamed creature as the Princess.

Shortly after being released from prison in Mandalay, Olive took Judy along to see the newest Doris Day film. It was a musical western called *Calamity Jane*, about a mischievous caravan trader who gallivanted across the American Wild West while dressed in men's clothes and told self-aggrandizing tall-tales at the trading post in Deadwood.

Calamity Jane and Olive were uncannily similar. They were both sharp shots, who wore red scarves around their necks and were brave on horseback. Just like Olive, Calamity Jane acted like a man and lived together in a house on the prairie with another woman. For days after the film, Olive was humming "Whip, crack away," Calamity Jane's song.

In the film, when Calamity Jane brought a beautiful songstress from the big city to perform in Deadwood, it resulted in such jealousy that it caused a brawl. Olive's girlfriend, prison warden Daw Htay Htay, was not exactly a brawl-inspiring beauty. So, Judy said, Olive decided to name her next horse Hurricane, after Calamity Jane's horse, and began looking for a different special lady to bring back to Kokang.

Also, right around when Olive was released, a CIA officer had identified Kokang as a good base for launching renewed subversive anti-communist activity.[1] Though the CIA had stopped providing direct financial aid to

Figure 10.1. Olive front and center, with "Fat Huang" Huang Dalong to her right. "Kokang Gregory Peck" is second from the left in the back row. Photo taken some time in 1956. YANG FAMILY PRIVATE COLLECTION.

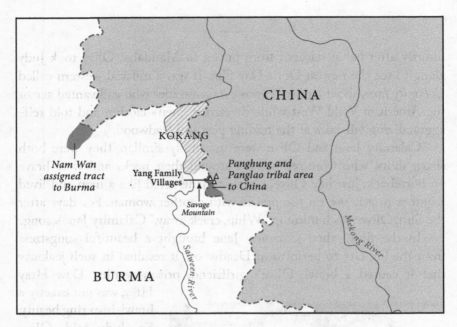

Map 10.1.   1954 China-Burma boundary.

the Secret Army, in Olive's absence, an independent detachment remained headquartered at Fat Huang's hideaway with a radio intelligence outpost.

Olive's Boys muled contraband from the mines and opium fields along the string of new Yang family villages on Savage Mountain and brought with them important tidbits about communist movements. The communists first arrived claiming they were there to protect the locals from the Secret Army, received airdrops of supplies, and now hundreds of them were garrisoned there.[2]

Harold had received word of an alarming development among the Wa on Savage Mountain: the communists had started building a road to the area there which had been undemarcated since Olive's one-eyed great-granduncle was ruler.

"The Reds are almost certain to take over old mining centers, and the Chinese have had their eyes set on that silver for the last fifty years,"[3] Harold wrote in a later report to his CIA superiors, concerned about the budding Chinese communist nibbling operation forming a ring of ten enemy communist bases. There were ten in total, reaching all the way to Kachin State, some as far as sixty miles inside Burmese territory where the border posts had yet to be set.[4]

The Chinese Communist Party, Harold feared, intended to stake a claim on Burmese lands, quite possibly the entire country all the way up to the Salween, including Kokang. With a border agreement looming in the future, the little string of Yang family villages and mines had turned into the last line of defense against what they feared was a Chinese communist takeover of Burma.

"The Chinese have no regard for any sort of an agreement and will use anything as a pretext to achieve their ends,"[5] Harold wrote.

The Borderland Poet occasionally sent agents behind enemy lines to middling effect. One managed no subversive acts in the three months he was dispatched to Savage Mountain—except to recruit one intelligence agent, who was a sex worker introduced to him by his predecessor.[6]

Figure 10.2.   Smelters at a mine in the Wa States in 1957.
BURMA WEEKLY BULLETIN.

So one day, Olive told Daw Htay Htay and Jeep that she had important business to attend to out of town and headed to Kokang with a few of Olive's Boys.

At the checkpoint in Lashio along the way, they were stopped by Sao Hom Hpa's men, who took Olive into custody. Olive had violated a no-travel order, so just to be safe, they deported her to Rangoon.

Once in Rangoon, she lost no time making a visit to the War Office, the Burma Army's headquarters, and managed to get a special letter of permission from a ranking general for travel to Kokang and to Savage Mountain as well.[7]

Sao Hom Hpa was shocked to see Olive ride into his court like a whirlwind, as she hopped off her white horse. Sao Hom Hpa's sister who was coincidentally nearby noticed a gun in both holsters at Olive's hips, and suddenly remembered: that was the girl who had brought a gun to school in her backpack.

"You know you're not supposed to bear arms in my court," said Sao Hom Hpa, surprised to see her return, so soon after being deported.

"I only brought them for you as a gift," Olive said, who was always quick on her feet with wit and charm. Olive offered the guns up with a smile, then she presented Sao Hom Hpa with the letter.

"It's illegal to traffick opium and to cooperate with Chinese brigands," Sao Hom Hpa reminded Olive when he looked up from the letter in anger. He saw Olive was accompanied by a soldier from Rangoon and a police officer. He had no choice but to follow orders. As he allowed her to ride on to Kokang, he knew Olive was up to no good.

By the time they arrived, the story of how Sao Hom Hpa was bested grew legs, and Olive returned to Kokang like Calamity Jane to Deadwood, with a tall tale of bravado to dazzle a group of cheering Olive's Boys.

"He asked me if I had a license for these guns, I told him I sure did," Olive crowed as she drew her guns and fired them both at once into the air. "Come get them if you dare!"

In fact, Olive was on a mission for the anti-communist "New Life Movement" in Kokang.[8]

The 101 garrison where General Li had once been headquartered in Kokang had ostensibly been turned into a school. Olive had gained utmost respect for her self-sacrificing prison stint and notoriety for her patriotic robbing and looting. There, the Borderland Poet encouraged their cadres to spread the word.

"Engage in the telling of heroic legends!" The Borderland Poet said. "Guerilla warfare is political warfare!"

All Kokang levies from their anti-communist guerilla force were required to attend classes. Their state guerilla force was supposed to be volunteers, but at the school, they were treated like a professional force who trained all day long. It was the primary reason they were so well known for being such good fighters. The instructors were strict and beat students when they couldn't manage the steep daily uphill climbs they were forced to do.[9]

Textbooks were hard to come by, but thankfully, the US embassy donated some from the anti-communist bookstore in Rangoon, which taught the principles of democracy and nationalism, and had Generalissimo Chiang's anti-communist song printed on the inside cover.

At the end of the day, they sang, "Kill traitors, kill traitors! Reclaim the mainland, save our compatriots!" They learned basic history and civics and that communist infiltrators could be legally shot on sight.

The US embassy had set up public libraries with programming designed to promote democracy and freedom and to trash the image of communists, including one near Jimmy's house in Rangoon.[10] They had a reading room filled with anti-communist texts, and their librarian remarked they couldn't keep enough copies of the wildly popular *How to Win Friends and Influence People* on their shelves.[11] They also provided publishing materials to community groups and lent out projectors.

After Olive was said to have helped bring the first projector to Kokang on mules, they started showing anti-communist films from Burma's psychological warfare department created by the CIA.[12] One was about a young man who journeys through the Burmese countryside to the big city in Rangoon after the Japanese invasion and learns about democracy and self-determination.[13] Evidently, they must have gotten their hands on films that were a little more fun, too: the most indisputably handsome levy at school gained the nickname Kokang Gregory Peck, for bearing a striking resemblance to the actor.[14]

Chinese communist troops on Savage Mountain were constantly making trouble with the local womenfolk. One day, two Wa women plunged to their deaths after encountering two communist troops near the border post on a mountaintop south of Kokang. They fell into the gorge below, near Fat Huang's route.

The communist troops swore it was an accident. They said they had followed the enchanting sound of two maidens singing a folk-song, but when they called out to the beautiful young sirens it gave them a fright. Coincidentally, when they were startled, they knocked into the border post, before falling off the mountain.

The next time there was unusual communist activity near the pillar, Wa assassins from Fat Huang's operation area enacted revenge. They captured and decapitated two armed communist soldiers, who turned out to be official border inspectors. The following week the Chinese government requested their return. Luckily, their skulls had not yet been cleaned and prepared for worship, so the chieftain instructed the communists' heads to be stitched back onto their bodies and returned in one piece. They were entombed in a martyr's mausoleum.[15]

Sometime in 1955, a group of three Wa chieftains just south of Kokang traveled to Kunming, carrying with them ancestral woodcuts, an elephant foot drum, and the skull of a gaur jungle bison. They received Mao's little red book and swore allegiance to the Chinese Communist Party. Then they attended a border conference, declared their territory for the motherland, and allowed the communists to start building their road through their villages.[16]

Among the Wa sympathetic to the communists was the chieftain of Banhong, whose decision would effectively cede the little Yang family villages near the mines and trading outpost to China.

When the first communist advance teams arrived, they were shocked by the primitive conditions in Wa villages and to learn there were a few large slave-owners, whose laborers were primarily engaged

Figure 10.3. Burmese customs officer weighing seized opium from a border crossing. BURMA WEEKLY BULLETIN, 1959.

in the painstaking work of opium cultivation. They judged the Wa slaves as generally lazy and disobedient. However, because the women were less likely to run away, they were more desirable. Both slavery and opium cultivation, the communists decided, would need to be abolished.

Harold had great confidence in the staunch anti-communist Wa, except for the tribe of Banhong. Even Olive's father had battled them when she was little.

"They can't be trusted," Harold later reminded his CIA superiors, regarding their past of allowing the Chinese to mine their silver.

"We'll use underground organizations to incite unrest in communist counties with our intelligence agents,"[17] The Borderland Poet advised for these sorts of situations.

The other chieftains banded together against the communist's road and threatened to kill any workers who dared build through their villages, forcing the road to take a wildly circuitous route around them.

An epidemic of smallpox had developed along the communists' new road, among Wa who had only just banished the practice of headhunting and were coming out of isolation. When communists came with medicine, Fat Huang haunted the supply road until even the teams of nurses had to travel with an armed team of escorts.[18] Someone started rumors in Wa villages that taking communist supplies was what gave them the disease and that they would be visited by death if they accepted them.[19]

Fat Huang's men threatened to rob and behead any merchants traversing Savage Mountain with any load of treasures from the Wa mines. When the communists sent a team of four to negotiate safe passage, they killed three of them and allowed one to live so he could return to tell them the horror of what he witnessed.[20]

In a Wa village on Savage Mountain that would ride the new border, a man claiming to be the reincarnated Buddha persuaded villagers to pledge support to the Red Chinese. Secret Army guerillas from Fat Huang's operation area went to retaliate against the chieftain, hoping to bully him into resisting the border agreement. It was said when they looted his home and beat his wife, they pulled her hair so hard it tore her scalp from her head, and her children all fled.[21]

Late in 1955, General Ne Win sent a Burma Army colonel with a regiment to investigate the communist base near where the two Wa women had fallen to their deaths. The Burmese troops had their Burmese flag prominently displayed, when the communist regiment attacked them on Burmese soil and attempted to take their vanguard prisoner. They clashed again hours later, killing one Burmese soldier before knocking a piece out of their border post during their retreat. Fat Huang's men remained on guard.[22]

But when a Burmese delegation inspecting damage from the clashes came to Kokang's boundary pillars near Fat Huang's hideaway, they threatened Edward.

"You have dutifully protected the frontier," the Burma Army commander began, commending Edward for defending their territory and not allowing the Chinese to move their border markers.

"And we have a desire for internal autonomy." Edward nodded in agreement with the Burmese delegation's praise, then reasserted the eternal request of his ancestors, not to be ruled by outsiders.

The commander had nodded politely and noticed Edward's sister, dressed in men's clothing, looming in the background, surrounded by a group of men who seemed to be under her direction. Olive was furious that the Burma Army hadn't done more to contain the Chinese incursion.

"Your frontier land is remote, nevertheless, Kokang is more politically advanced than other states we have visited," the commander said. But moments later, he pulled Edward aside, where Olive couldn't hear his threat.

"You think Kokang is made of steel? Steel can rust, you know."[23]

One day, one of Olive's students was arrested by Sao Hom Hpa's immigration officials, on suspicion of being a communist infiltrator from China. Edward went to bail him out and furnished him with a special letter bearing the Yang family seal. When he tried again to travel along the same route the following week, the letter didn't work. He was taken into custody again, because his identification papers had not been federally issued.

"I'm a Kokang native, the *sawbwa* can attest," he pleaded.[24] The accusation was insultingly racist, given his anti-communist indoctrination, and reeked of injustice and harassment. Olive started a campaign that began in whispers and ended in a grassroots civil rights movement unlike anything Kokang had ever seen.

Olive asked pertinent questions, such as, "How could someone in Rangoon know better than we, who is a Kokang native, and who is not?"

When a new Burmese police officer finally arrived to take his post in Old Street Village that winter, a group of a few hundred Kokang students started marching past the building with banners and posters that read "We are Burmese Nationals," and "Resist the Dictatorship." Fat Huang's sons, and Kokang Gregory Peck, and all the students from the 101 garrison chanted the words "Democracy and Rights!" as the newly arrived Burmese officer barricaded himself inside the police station

They marched from there to the edge of Kokang, where they boarded a fleet of jeeps Olive arranged, and started demonstrating along the trade routes that passed through the Kachin villages where Duan lived, all the way to the big trading post at the border. More followers joined, mostly merchants who were sick of being hassled by trade officials for bribes. By the time they passed Sao Hom Hpa's court near the government offices in Lashio, the crowd had grown. It was hard to say who was Kokang, and who was not, but it was clear that all were following Olive.

"Our compatriot has been wrongly jailed!" Olive called out to government officers in Lashio, spearheading the crowd cheering near the jail's entrance.[25] They hung around Lashio, making trouble until he was released. That week, Olive observed a patron at a tea shop there harassing a Chinese compatriot, and Olive's Boys started a streetside brawl. Then one of Olive's Boys wrote a letter to the editor of a newspaper, decrying the Chinese being treated as second-class citizens, following the fracas.[26]

Armed communist officials were constantly surreptitiously crossing the border in Kokang to arrest Olive's Boys. On one occasion, one of the thieves from Fat Huang's hideaway was accused of robbery and taken back to China. Party officials then sent an order to the Yang family court demanding the remaining bandits be handed over.

Olive, feeling the order challenged her sovereignty, charged the officials with trespassing and kidnapping and sent Fat Huang and the Ponytailed Bandit to shout insults at them at the border crossing, threatening to arrest them.[27] Because the communist officials wouldn't turn themselves over, Olive took her anger out on her own boy, the unfortunate messenger who carried the order.

"You, bandit-spy!"[28] Olive, who held no legal position in government, angrily accused him. "You should go to jail for such an act of sedition."

Fat Huang was said to have put the young man in a hole with a cage behind Olive's house instead of regular jail, and none of his relatives knew where he was.[29]

At first, General Ne Win had tried to keep the communist bases on Burmese soil a secret. But within a year, a local newspaper, *The Nation*, ran stories about the incident near Fat Huang's border post. Because the paper's publisher was Jimmy's friend, people wondered if he hadn't leaked the news.[30]

By 1955, the Voice of America, after an hour of jazz, picked up on the news stories of the communist incursion in northern Burma. There was widespread outrage that the Burmese Army hadn't done more to expel the communist intruders in the year since.[31] Down at Jimmy's house in Rangoon, when the siblings spent time together in the evenings, they often listened to the wildly popular Voice of America radio programs. They were produced from a studio at the US embassy and started with a whole hour of relaxing jazz before the news came on.[32] Afterward, they would sometimes listen to Radio Peking, who decried the anti-communist incursion.[33]

Not long after the stories ran, the communist regiment withdrew from their base on Savage Mountain. The Kokang guerillas considered it a massive victory—but amid celebrations, Olive suddenly received an order for deportation from Sao Hom Hpa for the crime of unlawful imprisonment.

By then, Judy said, one of their cousins had been pleading with Olive to set her prisoner free for nearly a month and had gone to complain to Sao Hom Hpa. Sao Hom Hpa finally issued an order to have Olive removed from Kokang and have the prisoner released.[34] Judy said Olive's prisoner, Peng Jiasheng, had already turned his heart against the Yang family by the time he was released, and that is why it was Olive's fault he eventually turned communist.

Before leaving, Olive entrusted Lo Hsing Han with overseeing security for the all-important trade route from the cultivation operation in the Hke Hpok villages, to a small illegal morphine processing plant and airstrip in the jungle on Sao Hom Hpa's land.[35] They say that when Olive bestowed upon Lo the great honor of this promotion, the future Godfather of Heroin first started stamping their processed opium with the "999" brand that would make him infamous.[36]

Talented smugglers like Olive knew to frequently change methods and routes to avoid being caught, so she set up a logging business on some land south of Kokang and began selling timber to Thailand through a sawmill next to a river. The river offered a convenient alternative route for opium shipments when the roads wouldn't do.[37]

Traditionally speaking, slave owners could exercise the right to kill their own slaves as the ultimate punishment. Olive was said to have run businesses like a dictator. Though Olive's siblings swore she never killed anybody herself, the murder of her deputy at the sawmill was a story oft repeated by those who feared her.

The deputy at the sawmill had been in charge of securing contraband that had been packed into hollowed out logs to be floated down to Thailand. When Olive learned the logs had gone missing before reaching their intended destination, she flew into a rage and summoned Fat Huang.

"Discipline him for failure to execute orders," Olive said, standing on the riverbank, astride the cowering deputy, surrounded by dozens of workers and men, who had stopped their tasks to witness what was about to occur. Fat Huang was said to have shot the deputy in plain view as a threat to those assembled, then floated his corpse down the river, as a warning to others downstream.[38]

Down in Thailand, four young Chinese men on the Chiangmai Express were caught smuggling what was ostensibly Olive's opium, hidden in frames of pictures affixed to the train's dining car.[39] The judge who sentenced them, a British war veteran named Gerald Sparrow, reduced their fines, because one of the convicts had suggested they may face potentially fatal penalties back in Burma during his plea for leniency.

Sparrow was a recently divorced nightclub owner, who was at ease among the criminal underworld that frequented and operated them. In Chiangmai, he had befriended the unrelenting opium smoker, Mr. Ho, who ostensibly operated a machinery export company and had an astoundingly well-kept girlfriend.[40]

Over drinks one evening at a nightclub with Mr. Ho, Sparrow learned the young Chinese men he sentenced were caught up in the police scam that had allowed him to operate undisturbed for several years.[41]

For any tips leading to an arrest, the Thai police offered rewards twice the value of seized contraband. So, Mr. Ho employed an informer, who occasionally ratted out his own deals to the police. When Mr. Ho's informer double-crossed his carriers, the reward typically covered the value of his lost merchandise. That was normally returned to him by the police anyhow.

"It's a brilliant if not unscrupulous business plan," Sparrow conceded.

In fact, Mr. Ho worked for the Taiwanese military intelligence bureau, had four aliases and passports, and worked as the broker buying Olive's opium through the Secret Army. Mr. Ho had mines as well and was dealing in gold and gems. On

Figure 10.4. Burmese actress Wah Wah Win Shwe pictured at age eighteen when she first met Olive.
GABRIELLE PALUCH.

his payroll, he bragged there were pilots, customs officers, the chief of police—even missionaries were working for him. Indirectly, the ministers of at least three sovereign states were in his pocket. Recently, Mr. Ho's stock had grown so large he was desperately looking to sell two hundred tons from his warehouse in Chiang Mai, more than an entire year's worth of what Burma usually produced. Some of it would likely go to Cairo, for onward sale to Europe or the United States.[42]

"That much?" Sparrow balked at the volume of Mr. Ho's business, underpinning the sudden unprecedented surge of opium traffic cases he had noted at his court. He noticed Mr. Ho's eyes had an evil glow to them.

"Larger and larger shipments have reached my warehouse. My opium agent is as beautiful as she is ruthless in directing all smuggling operations north of the border through her teams of assassins and has gained access to new fields in Burma and beyond," Mr. Ho said.

He described little hillside jungle airfields they had built in northern Burma, and even in Laos, that had allowed them to expand operations. Indeed, Mr. Ho's superiors from Taiwan had sent Secret Army reinforcements by plane; the Burma Army tried in vain again to drive them out, but they besieged Tachilek, a Burmese town at the heart of the Golden Triangle, near where the borders of Burma and Thailand meet Laos. They reached an uneasy peace agreement that April and were allowed to reestablish an opium trading post right on the river. Olive's old friend General Li had continued trading from there.[43]

"My opium agent in Burma is a nobleman's daughter, a princess of untold beauty who was banished from her home," Mr. Ho told Sparrow with a wink, knowing Sparrow's proclivities for beautiful women of Asian descent.

"Where is she?" Sparrow was instantly besotted with the idea of the woman Mr. Ho had described.

"Oh, I've never even met her myself, I've only ever heard from her agents," Mr. Ho said, before inviting Sparrow for a getaway on one of his planes. "You should see how beautiful the women are up there sometime."

Sparrow desperately wanted to meet an enchanting ruthless princess, so he started looking for Olive while also gathering evidence for narcotics authorities on Mr. Ho's smuggling ring. He asked anybody he could in Chiangmai about the beautiful opium princess. He played golf with the CIA station chief, flew on Dutch's plane, and even had an audience with Harold.[44]

It may very well have been Harold who told Sparrow of the wild tribe of assassins in Burma's Wa borderlands with China who desperately needed to be ruled. It was Harold, who was most knowledgeable about the unique customs, religion, flora and fauna of the border region that were being lost as they came in contact with modern society. And by 1957, as Sparrow was searching for Olive, Harold had decided to retire from the CIA so he could more fully devote himself to his zoo. Harold was so consumed with shame and guilt over his own role in taming the wild Wa, so he rarely spoke about the tribespeople he knew so uniquely well to his grandchildren, and they never learned what became of the magical iron staff the Wa bequeathed him.

But given the right company, like Sparrow, Harold spoke fondly of his time among the wild tribespeople, especially all the drunken feasts and sexually uninhibited tribeswomen of what his wife termed his "mid-life crisis."

Harold's sons Gordon and Bill remained loyal to the cause of keeping the Wa free of communism and established a new base outside of the zoo, in a temple on a mountain overlooking the border with Laos just north of Chiang Mai. Before Harold departed the agency, he prepared one last report to his CIA superiors, regarding the imminent threat the Chinese opium eradication campaign would present to the Wa way of life.

"If the Wa do not receive some material aid, the country will be lost," Harold wrote, trying to impress upon them how effectively the fierce Wa could foible the communist's plans—he reckoned they could hold out for a few years. He was certain there would be a Chinese invasion. "From present reports there is little doubt in my mind but that something major has already started."[45]

Harold's report was correct. Also that year, a British journalist working for a communist newspaper ventured among the tribespeople of Harold's beloved virgin jungles and concluded it was a rotting backwater of human life strictly in need of cleansing. The opium orgies and piles of silver ingots that were the privileges of the upper-class would have to be relinquished, as the communists decried the indulgent pleasures that came at the expense of slaves who toiled under their masters in the villages. Communist party officials started offering low-interest loans to debt-slaves engaged in opium cultivation—a threat to Olive's business model.

Judy said if you ever needed to borrow money from Olive, the best time to ask was just after the American pilots came with Mr. Ho's weekly shipments of gold to the airport in Rangoon. Olive's Boys would come barreling through the gates in trucks to Olive's new home just down the road from Jimmy's and would unload the treasure. Olive was exceedingly generous after the trucks came by and would show up at Jimmy's house with gifts like watches for all the siblings. Jimmy was running a private investment bank where Shan chieftains held their gold deposits and even helped Olive with her business licenses.[46]

Olive also liked to go over to Jimmy's house whenever Louisa Benson came over. Louisa was the heart-stoppingly beautiful, recently crowned Miss Burma at the first nationwide beauty contest. She frequently visited Kenneth, their mild-mannered and handsome younger brother, who was her classmate in high school. Olive would show up on the porch like clockwork, just to see Louisa come and go.

One day, Olive presented Louisa with a flattering gift, as she was leaving the house. It was Olive's standard seduction technique. When Olive turned around, Kenneth was standing there, smiling like a fool.

"What are you smiling about?" Olive asked.

"Oh, nothing," Kenneth replied. "But I don't think that gift will work."

"What do you mean?" Olive asked, angered.

"Louisa isn't in love with you; besides, you're a girl," Kenneth said smugly, having privately professed romantic feelings to Louisa, which were requited.

Olive fell into a rage in the foyer, kicking over the table. When Jean heard gunshots, she came running in to find Kenneth crouched behind the table, afraid to come out and face Olive, who was waiting for him with a cocked pistol, urging him to come out, "like a man."

For over a week, everybody was on edge, and Olive was inconsolable.

"Why do the women I love always love my brothers?" Olive had said to Kenneth, when apologizing for nearly shooting him.

Of anybody in the house, it was Jean who was best equipped to understand why Olive was so blue. She remembered how Olive had felt betrayed at her decision to marry Jimmy, and knew Olive was still resentful.

"Forget Louisa," Jean told Olive, remembering another beautiful girl, who had been at the same beauty contest with Louisa, "I'll introduce you to someone even better."

Down a winding lane in Rangoon's Golden Valley, they pulled up to the home of Wah Wah Win Shwe, a courteous and demure fifteen-year-old, whose mother thought little of her aspirations to fame. Wah Wah accepted a small gift Olive brought, and they were soon on their way with little fanfare.

In Olive's mind, they had begun a sort of patronage and courtship, so she regularly returned to discreetly deliver gifts without attracting attention from Wah Wah's mother. Until one day, Wah Wah received a phone call from a director who had seen her at the beauty contest, with an offer to be cast in a film.

"My mother won't let me be in a film!" she cried when Olive next showed up at her house with a gift. "My mother wants me to go to medical school!"

Olive promised Wah Wah to be her patron and to dutifully reassure her mother of her safety as her personal security guard. Judy was convinced Olive had threatened the director until he gave Wah Wah the role, just so that she could drive Wah Wah around.

"You were born to be a star," Olive told Wah Wah, then bought her a yellow Chevrolet, and began taking her to and from set.[47]

Judy said that was the time when Olive had a pearl in every harbor. At one time, she was even running cabaret shows with beautiful singers in the gambling dens around town.

Up in Kokang, a building in Old Street Village was turned into a middle school for girls, run by women teachers. The one hundred students who enrolled easily doubled the number of local women who could read in one fell swoop.[48] The day doors opened some of the Kokang headmen believed it was sheer madness.

"This would never have happened when their father was still alive," the headmen said.

Though Olive was not supposed to travel, Judy said she accompanied the students on a two-week field trip distributing leaflets promoting free women's education in Kokang, looking for more to enroll, just so she could recruit new girlfriends. Those days, young women were liable to be snatched at any time, Judy said. Especially if they had long hair that could be easily cut, so a witch-doctor could cast a spell on them.

As Olive's illicit opium from Burma kept pouring into Thailand's opium dens by the ton, so did a variety of women of Asian ethnicities at Mr. Ho's nightclubs. Sparrow examined Olive's criminal record and

Figure 10.5. A mobile reading room from the US embassy's libraries, part of the US Information Agency's anti-communist propaganda efforts in 1957.
US NATIONAL ARCHIVES.

fantasized about her in his dr in an intimate manner. He searched for her among gangsters and the singing cabaret girls.

Mr. Ho eventually invited Sparrow on a weekend getaway to Singapore, during which he expected to spend the weekend meeting exotic, beautiful women. Instead, Mr. Ho made Sparrow a panicked business proposition and offered a handsome salary in exchange for legal services. Sparrow swore he politely declined. Not too long thereafter, he retired. Sparrow reported Mr. Ho to narcotics authorities and promptly returned to England rightfully frightened for his life.[49]

Mr. Ho was remarkably powerful and largely controlled the four hundred tons of opium moving through Thailand annually. Sparrow told them about the opium and gold smuggled in the meat and the pilots and police payoffs. He expected pandemonium in his wake, but Mr. Ho's police chief was ousted in a coup instead. SEA Supply was dismantled, and the CIA opened new front companies and eventually renamed their airline Air America.

Sparrow's raunchy novel about Olive, *Opium Venture*, was published and became a hit as a legion of prurient servicemen began amassing in Thailand to resist the approaching Chinese communist tide, ravaging the Burmese countryside.[50] Though the United States had not yetofficially entered a conflict in Southeast Asia, a large number of clandestine servicemen known as "sheep-skippers" began passing through the new base which Harold's sons were operating.

Those men likely knew Sparrow's opium princess by a different name.[51] It's unclear exactly where the nickname originated, but a number of Harold's local recruits who knew Olive's efforts had gone a long way toward containing the communist infiltration on Savage Mountain, called her *Nang Kha Khon* in the Shan language, or "Miss Hairy Legs." Not even Olive's closest family members were familiar with the name, because the Shan dialect was unfamiliar to them.

CHAPTER ELEVEN

Call Me Uncle

"ARE YOU OK FOR FRIDAY?" JUDY TURNED TO ME ONE DAY WHILE I WAS visiting her. "Olive's stepson is out of town, Gabby, but the maid will let you in on Friday."

Judy looked satisfied with herself. The opportunity to meet Olive while her frightening stepson was out of town seemed too good to be true.

"When you go, be sure to ask Olive for some of these diapers for me. She always has a lot of diapers, they are cheaper there. You should bring her some too."

In *Opium Venture*, Gerald Sparrow trekked for thirteen days through the jungle with a flatulent elephant and an armed guard on a two-hundred-mile opium caravan route on his way to the Princess, wading through rivers and sleeping under the stars along the way. I flew to Lashio and rented a motorbike for the onward journey, carrying diapers and cigarettes as gifts.

At the courtyard where Olive had once threatened a classmate with a gun at the Guardian Angel's Convent, I started down the dusty road, toward a mahjong parlor upstairs from a Chinese school in the Kokang Cultural Association Building, where Olive had once been a member.

Then, I passed the house where the Yangs once lived just as Judy described it, next to a teashop on the hill, where Olive had once brawled.

This time, knowing it was one of Olive's former routes, I took my time on the road to Muse and passed through Salween Village, where Kokang soldiers who had remained loyal to Lo Hsing Han now lived.

Rising up out of the valley near Lashio into the hills adorned with pagodas, I frequently passed caravan traders on bikes, operating the same routes Olive had once operated.[*]

It was no elephant, but I could feel the undeniable thrill of the open road and the wind in my hair, and the hillsides were lush and green, revived by the mango rains of the monsoon season. Nevertheless, on the approach to Muse I felt a little bereft that it was the wrong season for opium blossoms, so I would see no poppies on the hills.

I knew I was unlikely to have an experience like the fabulist Gerald Sparrow, who learned all Olive's secrets and then glimpsed her moon-flowers. It had occurred to me that I may very well not be able to ask Olive any personal questions. I knew I was going to meet someone under the protection of a powerful militia leader, but it hadn't occurred to me that I was heading for an armed garrison.

Judy hadn't mentioned it—she had only mentioned the diapers.

For the last leg of the journey, I hired a car to better cope with the steep climbs. Judy had given me directions to what she called a "cow company," near Muse's border crossing on the northern edge of town. I knew I was in the right place when I started seeing livestock the color of gunmetal steel stalking the dusty fields between buildings.

I knew that if Olive was anything like her sister, we would get along just fine. But just in case I only got to ask her one question I was ready.

Nobody really seemed to know what Olive's gender was and when-ever they had an answer it seemed they had never bothered to ask. Because it would have been undoubtedly perceived as disrespectful to ask Olive's gender in a straightforward manner, I decided the best question to ask was, "How should I respectfully call you?"

---

[*] Zhang Wenqin Jade Dreams, Poppy Fields Collecting opium, Caravans Transformed into Motorcycle Convoys—The story of the border crossing between China, Myanmar, and Thailand, 陈丙先 木姐华人社会的形成, Feb. 25, 2021.

Figure 11.1.   Olive Yang, June 2015, at her stepson's home.
GABRIELLE PALUCH.

Eventually, I came upon a cattle depot, behind a Chinese-style white-tiled compound, and the car was directed to enter through a gate. As far as I knew, I was entering the home of a livestock exporter.

In fact, the cattle depot was Duan's disguised militia headquarters. I gathered myself, got out of the car, and as soon as I looked up, there Olive was, in a wheelchair, on the porch overlooking a large open yard. That's the moment they realized an American had breached the compound.

As I approached the porch with gifts and a voice recorder, they suddenly rolled Olive away. The assembled women who had previously been awaiting me in their pajamas rushed inside and got dressed. A man with a cherubic face came striding toward me, as people piled into cars and escaped.

He took a broad stance in front of me and then gently lifted his shirt to reveal a holstered gun. As he reached for his waist, I wasn't sure if the gesture was a threat or not. Then he drew the gun, setting it down on the table next to me, as he seated himself, and indicated I should sit down at the table with him.

I was trying to smile politely, but I assume that the face I made was one of sheer terror. He apologetically asked me who I was, as he kept his hand on his gun on the table.

"Are you armed?" He asked, without offering to introduce himself. "Who are you?"

"No, I'm not armed," I responded, showing him my voice recorder. "I'm the American journalist from before, and I was hoping to talk to your elder to ask permission to write a book."

After some tense discussion with a small group of men who had assembled, I tried to ask him who he was. "Are you Duan? Did we speak on the phone?"

My question was ignored. A protective line of soldiers formed from the door to the table, and Olive was rolled back out in a wheelchair.

Olive was frail and tiny, wearing a jade necklace and smoking a cigarette, smiling contently as the surrounding commotion unfolded.

"Are you Olive Yang?" I asked.

Figure 11.2.   Olive Yang, smoking on her stepson's porch, with her injured hand, in 2015.
GABRIELLE PALUCH.

A pretty, long-haired nursemaid repeated everything I said loudly into Olive's ear.

"Yes, I'm Olive Yang!" Olive replied, and gestured for me to sit.

I was too stunned to speak and began handing her the gifts I brought, the cigarettes and the diapers. Olive wanted to know where I was staying, whether I would join them for dinner, and why I had come.

"Judy says hello, she's the one who told me about you," I explained. "I'm a journalist, and I'd like to write about your life. Is that ok?"

"Many people have written about me," Olive said, apparently confused by the question. "What do you want to say?"

"I wanted to know," I began, trying to find the right words to ask, "how should I respectfully call you?

"Please," Olive said, "call me Uncle."

The protective line of men around Olive had grown increasingly uncomfortable and started to gesture to get me out of the compound.

"That's enough," one said and began to wheel Olive back inside the house. Once she was out of sight, I started to feel uneasy.

More men started filing in to the compound from the gate, I immediately began to rise from my chair, as I realized they, too, were armed. They brusquely escorted me away to my vehicle and advised me not to return.

CHAPTER TWELVE

A Shame to Earn Great Riches

THE TALE OF THE FEUDING YANG SIBLINGS GREW SO TWISTED, NOT EVEN THEIR trustiest deputies could keep track of the score. The way some heard the story: after ousting her own brother in a coup, Olive's final downfall resulted from an escalating disagreement over gambling debts. Jimmy had tipped off the police to usurp his own sister's business empire.[1]

Others believed Olive had quite delusionally petitioned a judge to legally marry Wah Wah. In a last-ditch effort to prevent Olive from humiliating the family with a prospect so absurd as a lesbian marriage, Jimmy had Olive committed to an insane asylum on the grounds that she must be crazy for marrying a woman.

The way Judy told the story, it was dictator Ne Win's sexual jealousy that spelled the end for Olive, and Wah Wah who played the ultimate rat.

Ne Win was a new dictator who liked them young, and asked his police chief to get him an audience with the hottest young thing on screen. But the police chief returned, frightened, with a threatening message saying Wah Wah had declined to see him.

"Who is this person, who dares refuse me?" Ne Win demanded.

"It is Olive Yang, the Kokang chieftain's sister, who has said she will not allow Wah Wah to see you, because she regards Wah Wah as her wife."

Though Ne Win had been battling Olive's Boys in one way or another since the beginning of his military career, this was the final straw, and he decided he'd had it with Olive Yang. Someone like Ne Win wouldn't allow himself to be emasculated. When the same police chief was sent back a week later, he arrested Olive.

In prison, Olive immediately set up a smuggling ring, helping other prisoners get messages or medicine from the outside. Olive devised a way to sneak food to a fellow prisoner in solitary confinement in a darkened hole, forced to drink water by sucking on a dirty wet rag for a month as punishment. Then, Olive landed in the hole for solitary confinement, and was made to suck water from a dirty rag, too.

Olive boastfully told of the day Ne Win himself came to Insein to gloat, and pulled Olive from the hole for an interrogation. Olive was tied in restraints, hadn't seen the light of day for weeks, and had never been thirstier.

"Speak," Ne Win had said, after asking Olive a series of questions.

"Water," Olive replied, forcing the dictator himself to put a glass to her lips himself, as she took a big gulp. Olive swore her spirit was never broken, and she asked Ne Win for water just so she could spit in his face.

"Dog!" Olive shouted, as she sprayed him. "You couldn't kill a man if he came at you with his foreskin out!"

The Chinese Communist Party officials were having a particularly difficult time eliminating slavery among the Wa, because nobody wanted to be identified as a slave-owner. It was insulting.

Olive attended a denunciation rally in a nearby town across the border, as a representative of the Kokang *sawbwa* family and was indignant to be criticized for being a rightist landlord and slave-owner after being accused of mistreating day-laborer cattle-ranchers. Chinese Communist Party officials claimed at least a few of Olive's followers had been kidnapped.

"Nonsense, when we sent cattle and workers, half of them died, and the rest came back with no hair," Olive said.[2]

Olive had been at work for nearly a year recruiting more followers. All around Kokang and beyond, they dropped leaflets that decried the *sawbwa*'s abdication as a devious communist plot to overthrow their independent rule. New defectors from China escaping the famines and anti-rightist campaigns of the Great Leap Forward flowed into Kokang for reeducation. Kokang armed ranchers had gotten together and let their cattle graze on the grassier pastures on their land past the border

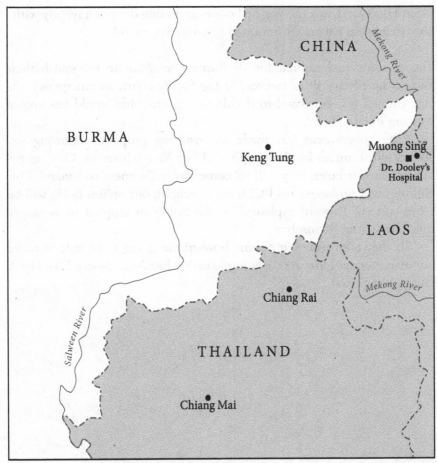

Map 12.1.   Location of Dr. Dooley's hospital

posts into China.[3] From there, they started snatching people and taking them back with them. When a Burma Army officer came to register households in Kokang, Olive started a whisper campaign that he was a secret communist plotting to arrest them. Just ten thousand people, less than a quarter of the population, went to get them. It left a great deal of unregistered people with no choice but to go underground and join Olive's Boys.[4] They went across the Salween into Duan's villages on Sao

Hom Hpa's land, too, picking up boys in gambling dens or anybody without citizenship papers who wanted to go underground.

The deadline had expired for all Burma's *sawbwas* to relinquish their ancient hereditary titles forever. At the family court, an emergency village council was convened to decide as a group what would become of Kokang in late 1958.[5]

"The government has made an insulting proposal regarding my abdication. I am to be the eighth and last Yang chieftain. Our courts, our police, our taxes, they will all come under Burmese command. Our children will no longer read Chinese in school; our opium fields will be criminalized," Edward explained as the headmen erupted in an angry murmur among themselves.

"If they take away our opium, how are we going to be able to make our own money? How are we going to eat?" a headman from a Hke Hpok village interjected.

Figure 12.1. Nam Tha "airport" arrival at a landing strip near Dr. Dooley's hospital where Olive's men eventually got weapons, 1957.
HALPERN, JOEL MARTIN UNIVERSITY OF WISCONSIN, MADISON.

"For too long, they have taken away our rights to self-determination!" Olive chimed in, from the back.

"The Red Chinese have offered us training and arms, and their maps show all of our ancestral land belongs to China," Edward said, calming the crowd as he continued.

Edward had been invited to a border conference together with the Chinese premier and been offered arms and training in exchange for pledging his ancestral lands to Chinese territory.[6]

"Defect to the communists? Never!" a voice rang through.

"In exchange for abdicating peacefully, I am to receive a cash sum in proportion to the tax districts as a retirement bonus," Edward continued.

"How much money is the retirement bonus?" one headman piped up. "I heard it was supposed to be a lot!"

Before Edward had a chance to answer the question Olive rose from her seat in the back.

"How much money, you ask? How much could be enough for my ancestors?" Olive said, then stretched out her arm, and pointed back to the gate of the family court, adorned with her grandfather's words. "Every man here today has passed through the same arch as I and knows it is a shame to earn riches without good strategies."

"We are prepared to fight!" one headman proclaimed, as consensus built in the room. "We don't need their money!"

All the men distrusted their Burmese administrators and were stirred by Olive's spirited speech. By the end of the evening, the Kokang people united behind the Yang family in resisting Burmese rule, having collectively decided to reject the retirement bonus.

All of Burma's chieftains would lose their right to export opium after the impending abdications. So Edward convened a meeting in Lashio at the Chinese elders' hall where they usually played mahjong.[7] A small group of disgruntled Kachin leaders shuffled in. They were from around Olive's former husband's lands, and many had been terrorized by Olive's men years prior. But they had just learned they would lose valuable opium-rich lands as a result of the border agreement.

As an alliance together with the Kokang, they could form a rebel army of 5,550 men, united for the causes of naturalization of Chinese citizens and the right to export opium. They leaned on Olive's help to get rifles from General Li.[8]

All the headmen's sons and Kokang's new recruits went down to a Secret Army base on the banks of the Mekong in batches for special training. Lo Hsing Han went, too, and they brought opium to buy rifles from Olive's old friend General Li's base.[9] It was in northwestern Laos, very close to the Chinese border in a place called Muong Sing.

The Americans had built a hospital there with a doctor named Thomas Dooley, which provided convenient cover for frequent supplies and weapons flown in on the CIA's planes. More Secret Army recruits preparing to mount an invasion of the mainland arrived.[10] The Borderland Poet thought of Dr. Dooley as General Li's excellent doctor, who did terrible intelligence work and foolishly hired double agents who interfered with their plans.[11] To his adoring Catholic donors at home who read his books, Dr. Dooley was a living saint who selflessly cured sick Laotian villagers. To his CIA superiors in Thailand, Dooley was a degenerate homosexual who was shamefully discharged from the Navy.[12]

When one of Harold's CIA recruits showed up with bags of looted funds at the hospital looking for weapons, Dr. Dooley said he swore he wasn't a gun-runner. More resistance groups came and an absconded disrobed monk with a few hundred followers.[13] Word reached all the way to the Chinese capital about guns at Dr. Dooley's hospital.

"In the region of Muong Sing the last six months under the guise of a medical team, the Americans have been inciting violence,"[14] a Radio Peking broadcast said, causing Dr. Dooley to fear for his life. Dooley was moved for his own safety not long thereafter.

"The Americans are plotting war in Laos!" the radio blared.

Up in Lashio, Sao Hom Hpa and a Burma Army officer summoned all thirty-three Shan *sawbwas* to be informed of their scheduled retirement and commuted pensions in February 1959.

"You want me to sell my ancestors on their land for a measly four hundred thousand kyats? That's simply not enough," Edward was said to have banged the table so angrily in the meeting, that Sao Hom Hpa thought he was drunk. "I don't need your retirement bonus. I intend to turn the power over to the Kokang people."

"Well, any refused pension can be refunded to the government budget," Sao Hom Hpa reasonably suggested, baffled by the display. Edward had been offered the same 15 percent of annual tax revenues as everybody else.

"If you don't resign, we will take Kokang by force," the angered Burma Army commander threatened. He knew very well Edward could afford to be so bold, because his menacing sister had assembled a loyal guerilla force behind him.[15]

Edward returned to his garrisons with Olive, reinforced their positions, and took stock of their weapons.[16]

Sao Hom Hpa donned his regalia for the last time with all the other Shan *sawbwas* that April, during the nine-gun salute at the retirement ceremony. Edward's was the only conspicuous absence. Shortly thereafter Sao Hom Hpa sent Edward an order to abdicate on risk of arrest.

Edward asked his top general, Kokang Gregory Peck, to saddle up for the longer journey to the Burma Army headquarters, where he would surrender to the commander-in-chief instead. His top advisor, Uncle Charlie, came, too. The confrontational meeting with the Burma Army's commander-in-chief General Ne Win was brief, as the siblings told the story. Edward immediately announced his abdication upon arrival.

"My people will not take kindly to being governed by outsiders," Edward said, reiterating his intention to turn the power over to the people. As a compromise, General Ne Win appointed Uncle Charlie as chairman of a local council to autonomously preside over their administration as a special frontier area.[17]

Edward left the meeting knowing he would be the last *sawbwa* of Kokang but took solace in the knowledge that he wouldn't be the last Yang to rule their land. The family's copper seal, issued by the last dynasty of the Chinese empire, remained in his hands.

When Kokang Gregory Peck returned to the family court, he found Olive was together with Lo Hsing Han, furiously plotting to reestablish their opium routes. Lo had barely escaped before a regiment of Burmese troops came in with heavy artillery units to seize their Secret Army morphine plant and airstrip on Sao Hom Hpa's land.[18] If they wanted to keep their logistics networks in place, they would have to fight. The Yang family's Kokang militia was a well-armed force of one thousand newly trained recruits with 450 new rifles, ready to protect their borders.[19] What followed was a series of ultimatums that carried with them the threat of death.

"Are you with me, or are you with the Burmese?" Olive asked.

"I serve the Yang family first," Kokang Gregory Peck said, kowtowing in the direction of their ancestor's shrine. Given Uncle Charlie had been appointed the new chairman, this was a true statement.

Olive, taking this as a yes, went with Kokang Gregory Peck, Lo, and a few others over to Uncle Charlie's house. As Uncle Charlie saw Olive's Boys approaching the family court, he remembered what his daughter had said years before, when the knife got stuck in her leg as she was cradling his grandchild. It was best to just stay out of Olive's way.

Olive was perhaps expecting to have to drink liquor with Uncle Charlie and reach a resolution before he got drunk; but before Olive could utter a word, Uncle Charlie had resigned as chairman, and Olive had taken his place on the local council. Edward had intended to turn power over to Uncle Charlie, but to the cursed siblings of the cursed eighth generation of the Yang family, there was no coup in Kokang. The power simply fell to the one most hell-bent on averting their fated demise.

Shortly after that, the Secret Army commander sent a letter to Ne Win threatening to join hands with Shan rebels.[20]

Gangs of rebels armed besieged towns all around the Salween River, fighting sentries along their opium routes, taking over statelets to loot their lands and people.

Allied Kachin units robbed communists of their uniforms and staged a feigned attack in disguise on Burma Army positions in Sao Hom Hpa's native town. They hoped to trigger a counterattack and fool the Burmese into spoiling their own border agreement. At first, the ruse appeared to

Figure 12.2. Insurgents who surrendered to the Burma Army near the Salween River, 1959. BURMA WEEKLY BULLETIN.

work when *The Nation* decried Reds had crossed into Burma and opened fire on ten Kachins—but no disagreements resulted.[21]

Then, they started to occupy some of Sao Hom Hpa and Duan's villages along the same roads as they had terrorized, still recovering from the terror of the last incursion just a few years prior. Again, they had to take up arms, many of them against the same soldiers they'd fought the last time.[22]

An evil omen witnessed by Kachin tribesmen—a four-mile long swarm of giant ants who spontaneously battled one another to the death—heralded the rebellion's climax.[23] When Burma Army reinforcements finally came to drive out the rebels to restore peace to the roads, they found weapons supplied by the Americans like the ones from Dooley's hospital and seized one of the Secret Army's mining operations. Amid the chaos, Burma Army commander-in-chief General Ne Win dissolved parliament.[24]

But no Burmese troops had reached Kokang's borders, and Olive arranged a hero's welcome for Edward. All the newly recruited tribespeople came to line the way in Old Street Village on the approach to the family court to cheer Edward's return as their ancestral patriarch. When Edward stopped to speak for the gathered throngs, he made sure to tell his people of his noble decision to refuse the pension, and they cheered their imminent independence from the Burmese.

"I have returned to turn the power over to the people, not the government," Edward declared. The Yang family's hefty financial sacrifice gave Edward's words extra weight that day. Villagers began to tell one another with pride of their leader's noble choice.[25]

Jeep recalled his mother's return to Kokang as unsettling, because everywhere they went, people were afraid of her. With Olive as security advisor, Kokang remained independent, but her greed knew no bounds.

Olive bought up all the tobacco and liquor licenses, taking a percentage of all sales in their state, then she extended the annual opium bazaar such that opium could be sold virtually year-round. The outlawed chain of gambling dens were reopened as recruiting grounds for Olive. Whenever gamblers overplayed their hands and owed money, Olive sent Fat Huang to force them to join the army until they worked off their debts.

Jeep began to feel embarrassed when he walked around with his mother at the mahjong halls where the gamblers looked ill. The trusted employees Olive had hired as callers were children picked from the youngest among her recruits, who weren't yet battle-ready. Jeep pitied the other boys, even Olive's favorites like Lo.

When Olive increased intake at their military academy, Fat Huang got carried away and threatened young children to come to school. Once they were there, instead of learning anything of value, they were treated like his personal slaves.

Meanwhile, in a Wa village of fervent Baptist believers, a few dozen chieftains gathered to make a covenant to fight the communists to the death around undemarcated borders on Savage Mountain.

To spoil the border agreement, the anti-communist guerillas arranged for the illustrious Wa chieftain whose seized letter got Olive jailed to be flown back to Burma from Taiwan on one of General Chennault's old planes to start feuds.

The chieftain started rumors the Chinese had come to mine their silver in villages where the people were divided, while chanting the Wa war cry, "Come help fight!"[26]

Just like their ancestors before them, feuds ensued among neighbors, killing one another in their homes in villages.

"The Wa are absolutely fearless and when incensed by some wrong will fight like wounded animals," Harold had warned about the Wa to his CIA superiors.[27] "Once on the warpath they don't know how to stop and have little regard for life or property," Over the following months, their granaries burned, killing hundreds more in the ensuing famines.[28] The feuds extended to the armed caravans of treasures and opium, in an endless cycle of retaliatory beheadings.[29]

In October 1960, the border south of Kokang that had been disputed since Olive's one-eyed great-granduncle was ruler was to be finalized, and the little string of Yang family villages where Olive had been cultivating opium on Savage Mountain were to be ceded to China. Their subversive attacks had been in vain.

Figure 12.3. Olive (eleventh from the left, just behind Burmese premier U Nu signing the document) at the ceremony for the Sino-Burmese border agreement, signed in Rangoon in October 1960. PUBLIC DOMAIN.

Olive wore a pale suit and black tie for the grand occasion of the signing of the border agreement in Rangoon, after which they would set the last border posts in Savage Mountain. They say that's when Olive caught wind of the secret agreement made between the Chinese and Burmese militaries to eliminate Secret Army bases, disguised as a border demarcation survey. A large regiment of Chinese troops from the communist People's Liberation Army would be allowed to attack major Secret Army's bases, for up to fifteen kilometers inside Burma along the border.[30]

Olive raced ahead to Kokang to warn Fat Huang to make sure none of the anti-communist guerillas perished as collateral damage and could abandon their positions. Among those who fled was the last remaining group of opium-cultivating Hke Hpok people in Kokang. Some of their descendants returned decades later but not to their original villages.[31]

Fat Huang, flanked by just his four sons, attacked the Burma Army unit before it had even entered Kokang proper, killing one of their soldiers. They say when they burned Fat Huang's house, his wife, sister, and daughter all perished in the fire. In his sorrow, Fat Huang was said to have gone on an unmitigated killing spree that included the Secret Army colonel he believed betrayed him.[32]

Further south, the joint operation drove thousands of men from massive bases, as they escaped across the Mekong River to safety at General Li's base.[33] A few weeks later, an unmarked Dakota plane sent from Taiwan dropped food and supplies, and Burmese Viper jets came thundering in from the west. They pursued the Dakota, exchanging fire along the way, until it crashed in Thailand.[34]

In Rangoon papers the next day, news of the downed plane aiding the Secret Army unleashed a flood of anger, and protestors flooded the streets between Jimmy's house and the US embassy. Within a week, a second complaint had been filed at the UN, and prime minister U Nu personally implored newly elected US president John F. Kennedy to help remove the Secret Army from their soil.[35]

A second US-organized withdrawal of the Secret Army followed—but General Li's men stayed behind again. Disguised as refugees, they crossed the border to a temple on a mountain near Chiang Mai where Harold's sons had established their training base for "Operation Momen-

Figure 12.4. Parachuted American weapons dropped by plane seized by the Burma Army during "Operation Mekong," part of the campaign to drive out the Secret Army in 1961. INFORMATION MINISTRY OF BURMA.

tum."[36] General Li's men overnighted in the monastery and learned to send Morse code messages over small portable radios.[37] They were hired as intelligence-gathering mercenaries who brought concealed radios behind enemy lines into Red China on their opium caravans for the CIA and became the first recruits of tens of thousands of tribesmen who joined the CIA's clandestine anti-communist paramilitary force to be deployed in Vietnam.[38]

The anti-communist guerillas remembered the Voice of America broadcast of President Kennedy, declaring that if "Lay-os" were lost to the free world, all Southeast Asia would be lost in the long run, too. They returned to their base near Dr. Dooley's old hospital, with the knowledge it was the most important front of the Cold War.[39]

Judy said sometime before everything started to go wrong, Olive had taken Wah Wah on a dazzling tour of her business empire, making sure every Olive's Boy had seen the most beautiful woman in the country at Olive's side. Wah Wah's first film had instantly catapulted her to enormous fame such that every man in Burma knew her name, from the family estate in Lashio to the sawmill down near their trading post. Olive was the object of every man's envy in the mahjong hall in Lashio like Calamity Jane at the saloon in Deadwood.

And after she returned from her trip, Judy said, young Wah Wah was taken in for questioning.

When General Ne Win staged the coup in March 1962, he hoped to put an end to the interminable insurgency in Shan State.[40] Police came to Jimmy's house and started disturbing things, taking documents and rare books that had served as irreplaceable records of the family's administrative history for centuries. Down the street, another Shan chieftain was arrested, and his son was shot.[41]

Parliament was dissolved again, universities suspended classes, diplomats left their posts; the Voice of America was forbidden from broadcasting, and newspapers shut down. Over the next few months, businesses that helped facilitate the insurgency were nationalized. Jimmy's bank and cinema were seized, and since he no longer held office in parliament he soon had no jobs at all.[42]

Olive was in a panic over how to keep the government from seizing her assets. So upon returning to Rangoon, she decided she would propose marriage to Wah Wah and then put the house in her name.

"Don't be ridiculous; you can't marry Wah Wah because you're a girl," Judy said, as they were seated on the porch together one afternoon. "Just give the house to me."

"What do you mean, I can't marry Wah Wah? You think I can't afford a ring?" Olive snarled.

"It's illegal!" Judy retorted, quite reasonably referring to the law, which stipulated marriages to be between a man and a woman.

"Since when has that ever stopped me from doing something?" Olive asked.

"Besides, Wah Wah would never marry you because she doesn't love you. She just wants your house."

Ever since the incident with Kenneth, Olive had been forbidden from bringing guns to the house, but the raging war of insults that followed was no less terrifying and resulted in a rift between sisters that lasted until they died.

After failing to convince a judge to legally marry them, Olive wrote Wah Wah's name onto the deed of the house and presented her with a splendid ruby ring.

In Kokang, Olive was making a killing after the socialist dictator's coup, and the subsequent shortages of everyday goods—the smuggling business was booming. As one of the last holdouts in the country that remained free, the only sign of Burmese rule was the small regiment of soldiers stationed near the border crossing.[43]

One day, not long after the coup, a Burmese sentry patrolling the market appeared to be interfering with people's purchases. It was unclear how the fight started. Someone started shouting in Kokang language, "I'm being extorted by the Burmese!"

Suddenly any able-bodied man in the market had leapt to his defense, first two, then five, then ten men overwhelmed the armed Burmese sentry. By the end of the brawl, he had been beaten to death by the market crowd under the afternoon sun, while Olive's Boys stood by and watched.[44]

General Li's caravan still moved freely to and from Kokang, The Yang family's Kokang opium syndicate was one of the few remaining legal exporters but had regularly exceeded its permitted allotment. Down in Thailand, US drug enforcement agents had been catching General Li's smugglers with 999-branded narcotics. Roughly one dozen of General Li's men that year, disguised as refugees, were caught smuggling eighty-eight blocks of morphine in Bangkok.[45]

Just after harvest season in October, Lo Hsing Han was accompanying a convoy of trucks in Tachilek, carrying 999-brand opium products from the Kokang syndicate, with licenses stamped with the Yang family's copper seal. He was expecting to take the load across the border to sell to General Li's agent.

Lo was taken into custody by border security. Before anybody could be notified, Olive's uncles, cousins, and in-laws were arrested around Shan State in a coordinated operation. Soldiers surrounded Edward's house in Lashio, knocked on the door and took him to their military barracks.

And finally, Olive was coincidentally alone at home in Rangoon the day the police came and threatened her guard with rifles as he opened the gate. Wah Wah was conspicuously out of the house, and Olive was taken by surprise.

Though Olive may have told tall tales from prison about spitting in General Ne Win's face, Olive's caretaker knew to be skeptical of the myths Olive told to replace the most tragic moments with tales of bravado. He suspected the truth of what happened to Olive in Insein Prison was a far more hideous story he only ever heard about from others. That General Ne Win had personally ordered a particular torture, perfectly designed to cruelly enact revenge on Olive.

After spending some time in solitary confinement, Olive was ordered out of the hole and into the yard in the center of the cell block. Then, an officer told Olive to undress.

"You say you have a wife, like a man? Take your clothes off!" he shouted, prodding with his gun. "Show us what kind of man you are, strip!"

All the other prisoners who were there were ashamed and said they shielded their eyes as they looked away. They didn't want to know exactly what was happening. But the prison guard who raped Olive shouted repeatedly that he would demonstrate what a real man does.

"She didn't tell me about that part, but then again she wouldn't," Olive's caretaker said.

Jimmy and Francis were the last two men standing of the Yang family rulers at the family court, panicked to find Olive had left their coffers empty. Barricaded across the Salween with a few relatives and headmen, their funds lasted about a year, until General Ne Win sent Lo Hsing Han to start a mutiny among the Yang's ranks. Olive, the master of whisper campaigns herself, had taught Lo how to do it best.

"Olive will come out soon to resist the Yang brothers," Lo told people in Kokang.

Francis said he cursed Olive's name, not knowing what torture she was experiencing, as he and Jimmy planned their escape to Thailand with General Li.

CHAPTER THIRTEEN

The Right Man for a Favor

FRANCIS

THE LAST TIME I SPOKE TO FRANCIS, IT WAS DURING THE DREARY WINTER months in England. He was battling a cold, so he made long pauses between sentences for his labored breath.

"Jimmy and I, we set off at night . . ." Francis began to tell of the eight-hundred-man exodus to Thailand in which they were forced to flee in 1964, after Olive and Edward were arrested. They joined a protected caravan of Olive's old friend General Li with their rebel army.

Once they had made it safely across the border, Jimmy was appointed co-commander for an alliance of purged Shan ethnic leaders as a Burmese government in exile. "It was one of my proudest moments," Francis said wistfully.

None other than Harold Young's son, Bill, was assigned to coordinate funding and training. Francis boarded a plane to Taiwan and described an audience with Generalissimo Chiang's son and visiting the airbase Chennault had built. When they returned to join the underground resistance in Thailand, they spent nearly two years in guerilla training in the jungle preparing to retake their ancestral homeland. After the fall harvest in Kokang, caravans descended to the border, carrying opium from fields that had once belonged to the Yang family.

But by the time Francis was ready to set off into battle as a commander together with their rebel force, he had fallen in love—and was saddled with an uneasy feeling of doom, that the family curse had already come to fruition.

"I knew when we set out, we were going to kill our cousins, our brothers. I couldn't do it." Francis said, tears of shame slowly swelling in his eyes, as he described his surrender in 1967. Francis's troops rallied behind a new leader among them: Peng Jiasheng, the young man whom Olive had wrongfully imprisoned. By the time Francis had safely returned to Rangoon, Peng had appealed to the Burma Communist Party for help on his way to retaking Kokang. Jimmy was left behind in Thailand with his men, who funded themselves by processing opium from the caravans that descended from the fields that had once belonged to their family after the fall harvest.

"That is how Kokang fell to the communists in the end," Francis admitted.

In 1971, the moment Edward died, when lightning struck as a torrential rainstorm came down, Francis felt the thunder claps reverberating with shame in his chest as he heard Edward's regret. "For a long time I blamed myself, and I blamed Olive, that Kokang was lost to the family. But not anymore."

By 1971, the United States had declared itself the global leader in the war on drugs; the war's architect, Harry Anslinger, had testified Chinese triads were to blame, citing the seized narcotics handled by the Kokang opium syndicate. The CIA had identified twenty-one opium refineries that were supplying the addictions of American troops in Vietnam, and they knew the kingpin was in Kokang.[1] That is how Lo Hsing Han was dubbed the King of Opium and came to be sentenced to death and was arrested soon thereafter.

"The Thai police said they raided his caravan—it was all fake." Francis said.

"What really happened?" I asked.

"He walked onto a helicopter of his own free will, even though he was sentenced to death. That's when I knew they were protecting Lo Hsing Han. The CIA, the DEA. All of them." Francis paused and gestured to my recorder, as if to remind me of my profession. "It happened right after a journalist delivered his proposal to sell opium to the US embassy."

"A journalist tried to help Lo Hsing Han make a drug deal?" I asked, sheepishly.

Indeed, a British journalist named Adrian Cowell had been following Lo's caravans for nearly a year when he hand-delivered a proposal to the embassy in Bangkok in 1973, to sell twelve million dollars worth of morphine—enough to supply every heroin addict in the United States for six months.

"I thought you would know about that," Francis said, puzzled, "maybe that's why Duan won't want to talk to you."

As Lo was arrested, Jimmy's men in Thailand started disappearing. Then, Jimmy too, was arrested in Thailand with a fake Taiwanese passport a few months later.[2]

Panicked, Jimmy sought asylum with the US authorities. By then, the CIA's Operation Momentum had produced a thirty-thousand-man army in Laos largely recruited by the Young family, which the agency swore didn't participate in the opium trade. But Jimmy knew very well that wasn't true: he had seen their training grounds and helped process and transport their opium.[3]

But the CIA couldn't help Jimmy anymore. Jimmy's arrest was considered one of the big counternarcotics achievements of the year, and it could send the Burmese authorities a strong message not to offer Jimmy asylum.[4] A top-secret message regarding Jimmy's extradition that passed Henry Kissinger's desk has yet to be declassified.[5]

Just when Francis thought things really couldn't get any worse, Lo Hsing Han was suddenly extradited back to Rangoon and put on trial in 1974.[6] Reporters lurked outside the courtroom when Lo started singing like a canary, describing an eight-hundred-mule caravan with nine thousand kilos of raw opium he traded to buy refining chemicals, uniforms, and weapons to fight communists and the Yangs. Judy had always known it was only a matter of time before he ratted Olive out.

Lo ratted on everybody: he bribed customs and police officers, military intelligence, even ministers. He described the payoffs and how they happened. He talked about all the opium he sold from the fields Olive's family once controlled to Jimmy. He said Jimmy's cousin was the one refining it into heroin, No. 4 pure China White.[7, 8]

Wherever Judy and Francis went, all anybody knew about them was that their family was famous for heroin, and they never wanted to think about it again.

Soon, the authorities raided Jean's house where Olive was living with Francis. They tore through their belongings and restaurant, accusing them of running a heroin trafficking scheme, looking for evidence. One officer who came upon a sanitary napkin in Jean's bedroom mistook them for medicinal patches. He quite intrusively helped himself and started marching around with one pasted to his forehead, then he arrested Olive who had to spend another few months in prison.

LIU

When Francis heard Olive's stepson Duan would not speak to me, he suggested I try a man named Liu Guoxi, who helped Olive pick up the pieces after the third imprisonment. Whenever Olive came back out of prison, the followers reappeared. One pretty young maiden even wrote Olive letters, begging her to be her master, asking to come live with her as her servant. Olive would go around calling in favors, asking to borrow money to restart her business. Judy had told me once Olive could walk up to anybody and ask for money, rattling off a list of nefarious businessmen who seemed forever indebted to her, including Liu.

On the phone, Liu was effusive as soon as I mentioned Olive: He first met her at school, perched atop her majestic white horse during sharpshooting drills as a young teenager. Liu was a bookish type but proudly called himself one of Olive's Boys, and invited me to his home in the capital, Naypyitaw, where he lived when parliament was in session.

"I would risk my life for Olive, it's important that she receive the proper care and respect," Liu said, perched on a white leather couch, dressed in blue silk pajamas and smoking a cigarette as we shared a pot of tea. "That's why I want to talk to you, out of respect for her."

Olive had been like a mother to him, even put him through school, but Liu was sad to admit that he began dedicating himself in such an unusually loyal manner to Olive, when he realized her biological son Jeep would not be there for her in her final moments.

"I am the son who will carry her to her grave now," Liu explained, grimly, because Jeep would not be able to do that for her. "Olive is our national hero, and her legacy must be preserved."

Liu lived in a sparsely decorated but densely guarded home and apologized for the inconvenience of making it through the gate. There was so much resentment about his taking office that he had twice been targeted in assassination attempts. He played an important role in facilitating the drug bust in Kokang that happened my first week in Myanmar.

The day the ceasefire was broken, Liu was the ranking deputy officer in Kokang. He had volunteered himself to lead the Myanmar government troops who came with the warrant for the arrest of his commander, Peng Jiasheng, the day of the drug bust. But Peng managed to escape east to China, and he remained vengeful and at large.

"Since the Yang family has gone, there has been no peace in Kokang, it's true," he said, echoing the notion of the family's curse.

Liu rather abruptly roused himself from the couch, stood with his arms out, and declared proudly that he intended to tell me the real history of Kokang, better than I had ever heard it before.

"You know, it was only with Olive's help in 1989 that we were able to negotiate that ceasefire. Together with Olive, Lo Hsing Han and I became the first to negotiate a ceasefire with the military government and opened the road to nationwide peace!"

"You were there for the handshake ceasefire? Weren't Olive and Lo enemies?" I asked. Surely, the man who betrayed her family and ratted her out to the court would have been on her bad side.

"I was there with Olive Yang, the only one who can keep the Kokang people truly united," he said, nodding furiously, hailing the deal as a sign of ethnic unity.

In 1989, the Burmese spymaster,[9] eager to take credit for putting an end to the rebellion, wanted to make peace with the communist rebel group that had occupied Kokang more or less since the Yangs had been expelled. He leaned on Olive's noble heritage to approach the communist rebel force, whose soldiers had come up under her tutelage.

Olive reunited with the old traitor Lo to meet them and convince them to talk to the government. The cast assembled at the negotiating table was an array of rival power players of the Golden Triangle, all of them Olive's Boys who between them had caused nearly forty years of narcotics-fueled insurgency. Olive was hailed for a remarkable contribution toward peacemaking.

But as Liu soon revealed, the ceasefire in question was hardly a mark of political progress; it was a glorified narcotics business deal.

"What did Olive do to help exactly?" I asked.

"Anything I know, Olive taught me," Liu said, crediting Olive with teaching him everything from how to load and shoot a pistol to setting up a shipping company.

There was really only one demand the Kokang rebels were making:[10] they wanted permission to set up a comprehensive trading company. As director of the company, Liu was to set up hotels and casinos and turn Kokang into a trade and tourism hub, using their legitimate merchant businesses as cover for illicit goods, just like Olive had once done.

"And then, Olive brought in the Duan family," Liu said, astoundingly, to me.

"I thought Olive hated her husband and never wanted to see him again," I was perplexed.

Liu laughed, amused at my disbelief. The Duan family's militia also controlled important shipping routes with adjoining territories— of course they would be included. "They have become very powerful," Liu said.[11]

Liu's wife entered the room, walked over to him, lifted his shirt and began administering an insulin syringe for his diabetes into his exposed belly. Liu continued to speak as if nothing were happening.

She then disappeared into the kitchen and returned with an armful of dishes on a tray and invited me to join them for dinner.

As we ate wordlessly in their kitchen, it finally made sense to me why Olive was being buried with Duan's family. Olive would die in peace, under the protection of one of the most powerful men in the country, in exchange for greasing his wheels along the way. The family was happy to accept Olive into their home when her hip was broken as a favor to a business partner, who had made them tons of money.

And Jeep would not be the one to carry his mother to her grave because it was dangerous for him to be there.

After New Year's Eve 2017, Francis's cold had devolved into pneumonia. He was suddenly hospitalized that February, and his son managed to rush to his bedside before he drew his last breath. By the time his wife arrived, heartbroken, it was too late. His ashes were distributed in Wales. At the funeral, they told the story of how he led his rebel troops to briefly recapture Kokang before capitulating. The whole family was stricken, particularly Judy, who wrote a death notice for Francis in the newspaper—but it was brief.

At first, back in Muse, Olive's nurse wasn't going to tell Olive that Francis died, worried that already frail with age, the grief would prove too much to endure. Indeed, Olive's tears kept coming. Olive stopped eating, grew weaker, then slipped into a coma that July.

"Olive is on her death bead," a text message from a family member read, "it's time."

The next morning, on July 12, 2017, the maid found Olive's cold body in bed; Olive had stopped breathing during the night.

For so many years, nobody wanted to talk about Olive, but by the time the funeral rolled around, nobody could stop. Hundreds of people attended the ceremonies—warlords from across the state attended, paying respects to Olive's corpse before he was cremated.

The funeral was so big, a week-long affair where they burned paper effigies of jeeps and of Olive's Boys. Women who had learned to read at Olive's school came. The elders from Kachin State came, as did the Wa. The inhabitants of Olive's old villages on Savage Mountain came. They shot fireworks into the night, as they sang anti-communist songs and hailed Olive's name. There was a nine-gun salute. The thought that Olive's death might have gone unnoticed seemed ludicrous.

Liu was among the men in the procession that carried Olive to the spot astride Duan Chao Wen's tomb, where she was buried according to their family's custom. Death notices in the Chinese press hailed Olive as a beloved leader. Listed alongside Olive's image, were dozens of members of the funeral committee, chaired by Lo Hsing Han's brother. He was keeping his dead brother's vow to pay for Olive's grand sendoff and headstone.

Olive's obituary, as published by the funeral committee, was so brief I was worried I'd missed something: "Yang Jin Xiu was the wife of the fourteenth chieftain of Tamuying, and died on July 17," it began and then ended with an elegiac couplet.

"Doffing armor and makeup to join the chieftain, a good mother of virtuous education, took up the sword and straddled a steed across the river, a worthy legendary heroine of the northeast."[12]

In Yangon, unable to attend the funeral because she was now too ill to leave the house, Judy cried all day. She had been crying since Francis died and could barely sit up without help. Her words were slow and quiet. It had been over a year since I had seen her, and her decline had been rapid. She had fewer teeth, her hair was matted.

"It's no fun when you have nobody to love. Now everybody I know is dead and gone."

My eyes welled up. I had seen Judy curse her sister, and yet she was overwhelmed with loss. This was a different Judy than the one I had known before her siblings were gone.

"I can spend some time with you," I said.

I offered to read aloud the obituary that had been published for her sister. She straightened herself out in her chair and listened intently, nodding after each sentence. At the end she asked me to read it a second time. She thanked me in a tiny voice, grasping my hand against the arm of her wheelchair.

"Thank you for this true story about my sister," Judy said. Before I bid Judy farewell, she told me she wasn't much longer for this world. She died a month later, in her sleep.

The day of Olive's funeral, around the graves of the first Yang ancestors near Red Rock River in Kokang, the rebel-held territories took the day off from shelling.

Jeep woke up in Chiang Mai and went to work as usual. He didn't want to talk about his mother or his family. And he didn't answer his phone, lest he hear from his half-brother. But when he caught his reflection in the mirror that day, and he thought of his mother, he noticed that things felt different. He went to the wall where he had tacked the letter to his mother and pulled it down.

By the time I visited him again, he had repainted the wall.

Notes

CHAPTER ONE

1. Peng Jiasheng, related by marriage through Olive's paternal aunt.

2. Myanmar National Democratic Alliance Army (MNDAA) launched an offensive in an attempt to take back the refineries and territory its fighters lost when they were purged during the drug bust just two weeks prior. "WY Brand Stimulant Tablets Seized" *New Light of Myanmar,* Sept. 4, 2009; Mahn Tha Sein, "Prosperous Future of Laukkai" *New Light of Myanmar,* Sept. 5, 2009. Mahn Tha Sein, "Prosperous Future of Laukkai (2)" *New Light of Myanmar,* Sept. 6, 2009; Maung Nwe Sit, "Kokang Region Remains peaceful and prosperous," *New Light of Myanmar,* Sept. 7, 2009; Ko Myanmar, "Reflected Glory to the Government," *New Light of Myanmar,* Sept. 8, 2009; "Drugs Seized in Shan State and Mandalay Division," *New Light of Myanmar,* Sept. 9 2009; Foreign Diplomats make tour of Laukkai *New Light of Myanmar,* Sept. 10; Tin Min Kyaw, "In conformity with transitory provisions," *New Light of Myanmar,* Sept. 12, 2009; Zaw Myint, "Tip From China sparked Kokang arms factory raid: gov't," *Myanmar Times,* Sept. 14, 2009.

3. Kokang Special Region No. 1 was the first special autonomous region to negotiate a ceasefire; the Shan State is the largest state in Myanmar with a multi-ethnic population and the largest number of ethnic minorities in the country.

4. It was disputed that the ceasefire had expired after a twenty-year term and that the Burmese army commander who was supposed to sign on behalf of his regional command unexpectedly passed before completing the paperwork.

5. 2021 coup leader Min Aung Hlaing.

6. *sarpei kenpehdaing* in Burmese.

7. Ross Dunkley, former publisher of the *Myanmar Times.*

8. "Raids in Rangoon Yield More Heroin," *The Irrawaddy,* January 30, 2009.

9. Aung Naing Oo, "Myanmar's Road to Peace" *Myanmar Times,* Yangon, Myanmar, Oct. 13, 2013.

10. David Lawitts, "The Transformation of an American Baptist Missionary Family into Covert Operatives," *Journal of the Siam Society* vol. 106, 2018.

11. Christopher Robbins, *Air America,* Putnam's, New York, 1979; Final report of the Select Committee to Study Governmental Operations with Respect to Intelligence Activities, United States Senate: together with additional, supplemental, and separate

views, p. 8: Richard Gibson, Wenhua Chen, *The Secret Army: Chiang Kai-shek and the Drug Warlords of the Golden Triangle.* John Wiley & Sons, Singapore, 2011, p. 12. CIA-RDP80-01601R001000050001-8 Dec 13, 1972.

12. "Battered Laotian Tribes Fear US Will Abandon It," *New York Times*, Oct. 11, 1972 New York Times; Intelligence Activities and the Rights of Americans, Final Report, Book II, p. 230.

13. Dennis Bernstein and Leslie Kean, "People of the Opiate: Burma's Dictatorship of Drugs," *The Nation*, 1996.

CHAPTER TWO

1. Gerald Sparrow. *Opium Venture.* United Kingdom: R. Hale, 1957.

2. Yang Jin Xiu 楊金秀.

3 Doom Burma's Robin Hood," New York Times October 10, 1927.

4. When Yang Guo Zhen's dead brother's widow was kidnapped by Chinese Muslim Panthay intruders in Wa State, he was injured and then dutifully paid high ransoms to get her back.

5. They were banished across the river to nearby Kutkai after a snap election held at the public bazaar after appealing to the British governor in Rangoon with funding from the Peng family. Yang Li, "House of Yang," Sydney, Bookpress, 1997, p. 16.

6. The Anglo-Vernacular School in Lashio.

7. The exiled relative was suspected to have engineered the poisoning through in-laws, Yang Wen Pin's wife's sister.

8. Yang, p. 25.

9. Yang, p. 22.

10. Their father, Yang Wen Pin, was *myosa*, or "eater of towns," an administrative position that came with taxation rights.

11. Kokang was gazetted, and the Yang family was granted an imperial government copper seal in 1840. The Shan States Opium Act of 1923 made the Yang family the sole legal wholesalers of opium in Kokang. In 1926, officially just thirty-seven tons of opium were produced in the Shan States; this was reduced to only eight tons over a period of ten years. Mi Mi Khaing, "Kanbawsa: A Modern Review," 1949, The Nation Publishing, Rangoon; "Untitled," *Eastern Daily Mail and Straits Morning Advertiser*, Aug. 6, 1907, p. 2.

12. Yang Wen Pin's （楊文濱）father Yang Chun Rong （杨春永） selected the couplet above the *yamen* (ancestral court) gate: "自愧筹边乏善策；唯期合邑庆升平" Yang Li, "House of Yang," Sydney, Bookpress, 1997, p. 16.

13. In 1739 Yang Xian Cai (杨献才) replaced the previous chieftain, who was surnamed Cheng.

14. Yang rulers were to dedicate themselves to the protection of their subjects, earning their support by being decisive, knowledgeable and experienced; while displaying quality of character with a moral sense of justice.

15. Yang Yong Gen was *heng*. In the late eighteenth century, when the territory was about half its present-day size, their land became known as Kokang. The name coincidentally began to suit the people who settled there. The word was originally derived from

the local Shan dialect, *Kau Kang* and meant, roughly, "place of nine guards." The Chinese estimation of the name, 果敢, can be understood roughly to mean "resolute courage." Htun Naing, *The Kokang People of the Upper Reaches of the Salween River*, self-published in Yangon, 2012, p. 45.

16. They called themselves Miao people, but in Kokang they were pejoratively known as Hke Hpok. The Hke Hpok (White Chinamen) are usually classified as a subgroup of the Hmong people, which were referred to as the Miao people at the time. *Gazetteer of Upper Burma and the Shan States Volume 1*, Part 1 by James George Scott, John Percy Hardiman, 1899, p. 597–98; *Asian Folklore Studies*, Japan: Nanzan University Institute of Anthropology, 1963, p. 84.

17. Yang, p. 16; The Shan State Act of 1887, Sai Aung Htun, *A History of the Shan State from its Origin to 1963*, Silkworm Books, Bangkok, 2009, p. 161; Khuen Sai, "Kokang Question," *Thai-Yunnan Project Newsletter*, Issue 12, 1991, p. 3.

18. Because opium was illegal within the British Empire, registered government buyers came to supply their hospitals with morphine from Kokang.

19. L. Puck Hee, "Travels in Kokang," *The Guardian*, Vol. 12 No. 5, 1958, Rangoon.

20. Godfrey Drage, *A Few Notes on Wa*, Superintendent Government Printing Press of Burma. 1907; Geraldine Edith Mitton, *In the Grip of the Head Hunters*, Black Inc. London. 1923.

21. The mountain range is known as Gongming Shan in English.

22. Harold Young. *Burma Headhunters*, XLibris, 2014, p. 8; 杨煜达 清代中期滇边银矿的矿民集团与边疆秩序 中国边疆史地研究. 2016, p. 4.

23. Harold Young, p. 27. Saimong Mongrai, "The Shan States and the British Annexation," Cornell University Press, p. 279.

24. 佤族历史文化研究. China: 社会科学文献出版社·人文分社, 2018, p. 53.

25. James George Scott, John Percy Hardiman, *Gazetteer of Upper Burma and the Shan States Part 2*, Volume 3, 190, p. 95; Sai Kham Mong, 37.

26. Gordon Young. *Journey From Banna*, XLibris, 2011, p. 55.

27. Sao Nuwadee Tinpe, Jane interview 07/2015.

28. Sao Nuwadee Tinpe, Jane interview 07/2015.

29. Harold Young, p. 19.

30. The widely held belief in Kokang was that to do so was to meet certain death, like the muleteers who returned from lower elevations with malaria.

31. Yang, p. 38.

32. Founded in 1908, Reverend B Massari, "Silver Jubilee of Saint Joseph's Convent," *Catholic Missions Vol. 15–16*, Aug. 1922. Society for the Propagation of the Faith, New York, 1927, p. 181.

33. Ronco, Daniele, "Il maggio di santa Oliva origin della forma sviluppo della tradizione," ETS, Pisa University, Pisa, 2001, p. 325.

34. The Shan Chief's School in Taunggyi.

35. Judy Yang interview July 6, 2015.

36. Yang, p. 43–45. Lu Shwin Zhen, Edward's bride, was the fifth of eight daughters to a civil servant in the finance ministry.

37. "Kunming Heavily Bombed," *New York Times*, Aug. 14, 1941, p. 4.

38. Curtiss Jack Samson, *Flying Tiger: The True Story of General Claire Chennaul and the US 14th Air Force in China*, Lyons Press, 2011, p. 183.

39. Interview with Francis Yang, July 12, 2015.

40. "Three Drives in Burma Push Back Allies," *New York Times*, May 5,1942; Yang, 63. IOR M/4 2955 HM Ambassador Report to Foreign Office 25th July 1944; Villagers of Bangyong went to pray for their safety at the Bangyong cave. It was dug by hand and had 1,700-year-old bricks left behind by a Han dynasty general who had set up a bivouac there and built a bridge across the Salween. Passersby who disturbed the bricks were said to be struck by a sudden mysterious stomach pain and unable to move. Passersby who spoke too loudly and disturbed the spirits would be suddenly caught in a rain storm. Whenever disturbances were on their way to Kokang, mysterious cannon-fire could be heard from the cave. So the chieftain went every year to burn incense, appease the spirits, and pray for his safety. Written by Claire Lee Chennault, Edited by Robert Hotz, *Way of a Fighter: Memoirs of General Claire Lee Chennault*, G. P. Putnam's Sons, New York, 1949, p. 64.

41. Ibid.

42. Yang, p. 49.

43. 93rd Division of the 11th Army under Chen Kefei from the KMT Expeditionary Force Chinese in Kunlong Under Song Xilian. Yang Wen Pin's first younger brother, 楊文燦 Yang Wen Can, trained at Dali and became an officer. IOR Burma During Japanese Occupation T10737, Yang, p. 51. A women's regiment was sent to the Burma border but Olive's name is not listed, for more reading: 中国远征军女兵缅甸蒙难记 By 革非, 1992,

44. Yang Kyein Hsiang on September 30, 1943, The Kokang Mutiny: Review of Events in Kokang, April 1944, WO 208/459 Yang Wen Tai. Paul H. Kratoska, *Southeast Asian Minorities in the Wartime Japanese Empire*, Routledge Curzon, New York, 2002.

45. Joannes Beamish, *Burma Drop* Elek Books, 1958, p. 179–83. "Flier Down in China," *New York Times*, Jan. 4, 1943.

46. Uncle Yang Wen Can, Richard Duckett, *Spiers Mission: The Special Operations Executive in Burma*, IB Tauris Co. Ltd., London, 2018, p. 162. John Beamish, *Burma Drop*, Elek Books, New York, 1958, p. 179–83.

CHAPTER THREE

1. BBC Burmese NLD ဝင်မပြိုင်တဲ့ ကိုးကန့်မှာ ရှုးကတောက်ပွဲ ဘယ်သူ အရေးသာမလဲ August 3, 2020, https://www.bbc.com/burmese/burma-53635092.

2. Allen Dulles briefing CIA-RDP70-00058R000100010051-3 April 3. 1953; SANITIZED CIA-RDP59-00882R000200200063-5 May 20, 1955; "Worldwide Propaganda Network Built by the C.I.A." *New York Times*, Dec. 26, 1977. Minutes of IAC Meeting CIA-RDP67-00059A000100110015-2 March 31, 1950.

CHAPTER FOUR

1. 程景. 金三角风云(泰国坤沙贩毒集团). 北方文艺出版社. 2018. Chapter 4.

2. Duan is referring to the local colloquialism for a love marriage, in which the husband and wife agree to marry before asking their parents' permission, suggesting the marriage had not been arranged.

3. 博尊宝 信仰如血 天马出版有限公司。2013. Chapter 17.

4. Yang Wen Pin remained in prison until April 1944, when he was released on condition he would wait out the rest of the war in the safety of a British hill station in India, in Kalimpong. His wife's heart condition prevented her from flying over "The Hump."

5. Yang, p. 21. The ritual of marriage was sometimes known as "stealing female relatives."

6. Yang, p. 26. They also raised taxes; farmland of fugitive households was transferred to retired soldiers; gun licenses were issued for those who had American, British, or Chinese arms left over from the war, and a small volunteer army of 150 was formed with remaining guns.

7. Yang, p. 66.

8. *Shaji* 杀鸡 Taungdwin Bo Thein, *Tamuying Mong Wong Ethnic Group and its History*, Lashio, 2003, p. 23. Accessed at the Lashio Museum for Ethnic Minorities.

9. On August 15, 1947, Yang Qizhi and Jimmy went to Maymyo to stand before the newly formed Shan State Council; the Yangs hadn't attended obeisance ceremonies since the war, and it had caused tensions among the families. Sao Hkun Hkio, the *sawbwa* of Mong Mit wrote the decision "The Secession of Kokang." Sai Aung Htun, *A History of the Shan State from its Origin to 1963*, Silkworm Books, Bangkok, 2009, pp. 233, 166.

10. Edward's grandfather held the title of *heng*, his father held the title of *myosa*. Edward was elected to parliament, and the Kokang were included among the list of indigenous races offered citizenship in Burma. *Sawbwa* is a Burmese word derived from the Shan word *chaofa* or *saopha*, which roughly translates as Lord of the Sky. The population was roughly forty thousand at the time. Sai Kam Mon, p. 43.

11. 蔡山 果敢志, p. 67.

12. Duan's village is called Tamuying. Their first ancestor was of Chinese descent and was rewarded his land and title when he gave the Burmese King critical military advice on his elephant-mounted advance to conquer Siam King Bayinnaung sixteenth-century Toungoo Dynasty Duan Wu, Around Kutkai, 方天建：缅甸勐稳华人身份本土化问题研究《世界民族》(京)2018年第1期; 段榮昌 滇籍旅緬三聞僑 雲南文獻第26期.

13. "Beautiful Bandit of Burma," *Melbourne Weekly Times*, August 22, 1948.

14. . "Jilted Joan of Arc Takes Revenge in Burma," Oct. 28, 1948, *Leonora News*.

15. Yang, 22; Sai Kam Mong, *Kokang and Kachin in the Shan States (1945–1960)*, Chulalongkorn University Press, 2011, p. 42; *Tamuying Mong Wong Ethnic Group and its History*, Taungdwin Bo Thein, Lashio, 2003, p. 23. Accessed at the Lashio Museum for Ethnic Minorities. Joint Sino–Burma Border Defense, *Singapore Free Press*, May 20, 1949; Yang, Bo. Translation by Clive Gulliver, "Golden Triangle: Frontier and Wilderness," Joint Publishing Co., Hong Kong, 1997, p. 141.

16. 黄大龙, Huang Da Long. 蔡山.

17. Interview with sister Judy Yang dated July 3, 2015.

18. 兔儿不吃窝边草

19. 李明富. 沧源佤族自治县志，云南民族出版社, 1998, p. 35.

20. Yang, 52–56; Information Report Background on the Chinese Nationalist Problem in Burma Dec. 8, 1953, CIA-RDP80-00810A003100860001-2; Information report, "Yunnanese Chieftains Pledge Tribal Support," Sept. 6, 1950, CIA-RDP80-00809A000600340320-8; 滇緬邊務及滇康印邊區劃界（二）020000000527A Ministry of Foreign Affairs1945/08/27, 緬屬果敢縣請入屬我國版圖

21. Sai Kham Mong, 78.

CHAPTER SIX

1. Bo Yang, *Alien Realm*, Taipei, 1961. Translated by Janice J. Yu. Janus Publishing Company, London, 1996, p. 125.

2. Richard Michael Gibson and Wen H.Chen, *The Secret Army: Chiang Kai-shek and the Drug Warlords of the Golden Triangle*, Wiley, 2011. Loc 1019, "The Battle of Tachilek." Information Report, "Chinese Nationalist Troops in Kengtung," June 27, 1950, CIA-RDP82-00457R005100430004-8; "Burma Seems Unconcerned over Reds," June 19, 1950, *Singapore Standard*; At a secret meeting earlier that year decided to form a guerilla force eventually called the Yunnan Anti-communist National Salvation Army but colloquially referred to as the Secret Army or Lone Army; Information Report: "Burma China Frontier Summary," March 1950, CIA-RDP08C01297R000100190009-4.

3. Yang, pp. 52–56; Information Report Background on the Chinese Nationalist Problem in Kengtung, Dec. 8, 1953; Information Report Free Yunnan Movement, July 10, 1950, CIA-RDP82-00457R005200570004-2.

4. Robert Taylor, *Foreign and Domestic Consequences of the KMT in Burma*, Cornell University Press, Ithaca, New York, 1973.

5. "Your Pants Please," *Sunday Tribune*, Singapore, Jan. 1, 1950; "Nationalist Troops Quit Burma," *Singapore Standard*, Sept. 14, 1950.

6. "Kokang" No. 2008/M4 Office of the Special Commissioner of Shan State, Dec. 28, 1950, Myanmar National Archives, Yangon, Myanmar.

7. Naw Seng, an ethnic Kachin deserter-turned-rebel.

8. Kokang's southeastern trading post, Chin Shwe Haw.

9. "Kokang" No. 2008/M4 Office of the Special Commissioner of Shan State, Dec. 28, 1950, Myanmar National Archives, Yangon, Myanmar.

10. "Kokang" No. 2008/M4 Office of the Special Commissioner of Shan State, Dec. 28, 1950, Myanmar National Archives, Yangon, Myanmar.

11. Alfred T. Cox, CS Historical Paper No. 87 History of CAT Vol. 2, April 1969; William Leary, *Perilous Missions: Civil Air Transport and CIA Operations in Asia*, University of Alabama Press, 1984, p. 110; Registered as a carrier in Taiwan, co-owned by a number of investors, including the CIA and Chennault, through a Delaware shell company.

12. The Defense and State Departments' $12.5 billion blueprint for the militarization of the Cold War, a top secret National Security Council report titled, "United States Objectives and Programs for National Security," April 7, 1950, NSC-68; *Report to the National Security Council by the Department of State Feb. 27, 1950*, No. 64.

13. The Southeast Asia Supply Corporation, a Bangkok-based shell company at 10 Phra Athit Road incorporated in Miami, Florida. Colonel Raymond Peers, formerly of

the OSS Detachment 101 commander in Burma during World War II, opened the office. "Mr. Ho" was likely actually a deputy of Li Mi. He replaced the original KMT government agent who lived in Kengtung for many years known as Zhang Fu Chu.

14. The CIA radio operators from SEA Supply went by Stewart and Marks; Leary, p. 130.

15. Edward had one of the twenty-five seats of the Chamber of Nationalities reserved for Shan *sawbwas* and appointed thirteen headmen. Yang Qizhi was in charge of government affairs, and Yang Zhenxin, Yang Wen Can's son, was in charge of military affairs. Customary laws were codified 果敢单行法律问答 was published Dec. 23, 1947. Mimeographs printed and redistributed by the headquarters of the Special Administrative Region Government on Aug. 11, 1994, and were preserved in Chonggang Township. Covering ninety-one questions and answers, thirteen thousand words. 蔡山.

16. Sai Kham Mong, p. 85.

17. Information Report Accessibility to Mong Hsat, May 26, 1953, CIA-RDP91T01172R000200300036-9; on April 10, future central figures in Taiwan's Intelligence Bureau of the Ministry of National Defense (IBMND) operations in Burma gathered; Information Report: "Chinese and BCP Activity," Dec. 10, 1951, CIA-RDP82-00457R009600070011-1.

18. *Kuomintang Aggression Against Burma*, Burma Information and Broadcasting Department, Rangoon, 1953, p. 181; "Rallying the Troops," Loc 2157; Information Report, "Military and Political Developments in Yunnan," Feb. 13, 1951, CIA-RDP 82-00457R007000060005-7.

19. Catherine Lamour, *Enquête sur une Armée Secrète*, Seuil, Paris, 1975, pp. 76–77; Ministry of Information, *Kuomintang Aggression Against Burma*, pp. 9–10; Information Report: "Guerilla Activities Yunnan," March 20, 1951, CIA-RDP82-00457R007200780010-3; Information Report: "Possible New Camp Site in Burma-Yunnan Border," Sept. 28, 1950, CIA-RDP82-00457R005900060005-0.

20. 金三角國軍血淚史(1950–1981). Taiwan: 中央研究院, 2009, p. 75–81.

21. The chieftain of Kunma, according to Catherine Lamour, *Enquête sur une armée secrète*, Seuil, Paris, 1975, p. 83;

22. Ponytailed Bandit 李泰興 Li Taixing. *KMT Aggression*, p. 11; Information Report; "Activities of Chinese Individuals and groups in Burma," March 13, 1951, CIA-RDP82-00457R007100550005-2.

23. Catherine Lamour, *Enquête sur une armée secrète*, Seuil, Paris, 1975, p. 83; KMT Aggression, pp. 10–13.

24. "US Led Nationalist Remnants in Burma," *Singapore Standard*, Jun. 9, 1951. Raymond Peers, OSS Detachment 101 Commander during World War II, directed operations from Taiwan.

25. 镇康县志. China: 四川民族出版社, 1992, p. 30.

26. Gibson, "The Airfield at Mengsa," Loc 2457.

27. They received $60,000 for salaries June 5; Daily Digest Intelligence Briefing April 26, 1951, CIA-RDP79T01146A000100490001-8.

28. Gibson, "PLA Counterattack," Loc 2509.

29. President (1945–1953: Truman). Office of the Personal Secretary. 1945–1953 NIA 207522846; Information Report KMT Activities in the Kengtung Area Dec. 1, 1951. CIA-RDP82-00457R009300510007-3.

30. 镇康县志. China: 四川民族出版社, 1992, p. 30. 覃怡輝 金三角國軍血淚史：1950–1981 · 中央研究院 2009, p. 87; Current Intelligence Bulletin, July 4, 1951; Information Report Possible Chinese Communist Invasion of Kengtung, August 15, 1951, CIA-RDP82-00457R008300560008-5.

31. 金三角國軍血淚史(1950–1981). Taiwan: 中央研究院, 2009, p. 87. Yang, p. 27. 覃怡輝 pp. 87, 441; Ministry of Information, *Kuomintang Aggression Against Burma*, Burma Information and Broadcasting Department, Rangoon, 1953, pp. 215 220. Appendix E, the headquarters of the central 2nd Army Division; Jan. 16, 1951; Oct. 13, 1951. Many guerila bandits in Yunan dare not go out Righteous China Information report Disposition of Chinese communist and nationalist troops along the Burma-Yunnan border. June 1, 1951, CIA-RDP82-00457R007900010011-6. Jan. 11, 1951, Information Report Chinese Communist Troops in Yunnan Province CIA-RDP82-00457R006500740008-8.

32. 雲耀宗 抗英英雄李希哲《雲南文獻》第十三期；民國72年12月25日出版.

33. Information Report, March 13, 1951, CIA-RDP82-00457R007100550005-2; *Kuomintang Aggression*, p. 213; "Invasion of Burma Not Confirmed," *Singapore Standard*, p. 7, Nov. 17, 1950; Information "Yunnanese Tribal Chieftains" Report Sept. 6, 1950, CIA-RDP80-00809A000600340320-8.

34. . 李先庚 "七載邊荒詩稿——滇緬邊區紀事" "雲南文獻" 第七期；民國 66年12月25日出版台北 In English: Li Xiangeng, Seven Years of Borderland Poems, *Yunnan Literature*, Dec. 25, 2006, Taipei.

35. Information Report, "Chinese Communist Dispositions in Yunnan," Feb. 4, 1952, CIA-RDP82-00457R010200430006-9; Information Report, "Military Activities in Burma," Feb. 2, 1951, CIA-RDP82-00457R006700440004-0.

36. He relinquished military ties, on the grounds that Edward was in violation of their co-defense sphere Sai Kham Mong. *Kokang and Kachin in the Shan Atate (1945–1960)*, White Lotus Press, Bangkok, 2005, p. 42.

37. Sai Kam Mong, p. 45.

38. Information Report, "Political and Military Developments in Yunnan," Feb. 13, 1951, CIA-RDP82-00457R007000060005-7；镇康县志. China: 四川民族出版社, 1992.

39. Jimmy lived at 137 University Avenue just around the corner from the Shan State government's headquarters. "Gunmen Hired to Win Vote," May 4, 1951, p.3, Singapore Free Press; "Burma to Defer National Vote," March 11, 1951, New York Times; Information Report: "Possible Chinese Communist Invasion of Kengtung," Aug. 15, 1951, CIA-RDP82-00457R008300560008-5.

40. Kenton Clymer, "A Delicate Relationship: The United States and Burma/Myanmar Since 1945," Ithaca Cornell University Press, 2015, pp. 91–96 ; "Current Intelligence Bulletin," Jun. 5, 1951, CIA-RDP79T00975A000200400001-4.

41. "Chiang Men Straddle Burma China Border," Aug. 23, 1951, Singapore Standard, p. 5; Seymour Topping, Journey Between Two Chinas,. Harper and Row, New York, 1972, p. 129; The Association for Diplomatic Studies and Training Foreign Affairs Oral

History Project Information Series, Morton Smith Interviewed by: Ed Findlay, Nov. 16, 1994, p. 14.

42. Before he bid his neighbor Jimmy farewell, Ambassador Key managed to reach an agreement to allow US scholars to study at Rangoon University. Soon, Burma had its first CIA director, and the first officers with unofficial cover began arriving. Among the first was Carleton Ames, who had a PhD in Burmese history and had arrived under the pretense of writing a book funded by the Ford Foundation. He brought with him his son Aldrich, who went on to become a double agent for the Soviet spy agency and compromised more highly classified assets than any mole in the history of the CIA. For more reading: Tim Wiener, *Betrayal: The Story of Aldrich Ames, an American Spy*, Penguin Random House, New York, 1995.

43. David Key, Foreign Relations of the United States, 1951, Asia and the Pacific, Vol. VI, Part 1 690B.9321/8–1551: TelegramPresident (1945–1953 : Truman), Office of the Personal Secretary, 1945–1953 NIA 207522846; Information Report, "KMT Activities in the Kengtung Area,"' Dec. 1, 1951. CIA-RDP82-00457R009300510007-3; Information Report, "Communist Troop Dispositions," Feb. 4, 1952, CIA-RDP82-00457R010200430006-9; Intelligence Report: "Burma/China," Oct. 11, 1951, CIA-RDP82-00457R008900100008-9.

CHAPTER SEVEN

1. One had even been arrested smuggling opium in Chicago, after being invited to the United States for CIA training. Justice Department Treatment of Criminal Cases Involving CIA Personnel and Claims of National Security: Hearings Before a Subcommittee of . . . 94–1, July 22, 23, 29, 31, and August 1, 1975. United States: n.p., 1975, p. 323.

2. Lo Hsing Han together with Hsu Wen Long, who had been village headman, started gathering Olive's followers.

CHAPTER EIGHT

1. 程景 金三角风云(泰国坤沙贩毒集团) 北方文艺出版社, Beijing, 2018, chapter 4.

2. Sai Kham Mong, pp. 68–71; Yang, p. 68.

3. The Special Commissioner Sao Hom Hpa issued export licenses to the Yang family for a certain number of pounds of raw opium each year around the time of the harvest, which they were allowed to sell to muleteers. Numerous accounts claim Olive was given a titular role of administrative commander and a cut of the Secret Army's taxes in exchange for allowing soldiers safe haven in Kokang. In the Secret Army's records, Li Taixing and Huang Dalong appear as column commanders.

4. 蔡山 果敢志 天马出版社 香港 2012, pp. 146–48.

5. The village headman there was a man named Hsu Wen Long, who apologized to Edward on his deathbed after betraying him with Lo Hsing Han. His son, Anthony Hsu, is still in Kokang government.

6. Hkun Shili, Ohn Kya Letter to the Special Commissioner of Shan State Myanmar National Archives dated Dec. 14, 1951, Myanmar National Archives Yangon.

7. Sai Kham Mong, 73; Information Report, "Opium Traffic between Mong Hang Burma and Chiang Mai Thailand," Nov. 12, 1953, CIA-RDP80-00810A002700970003-3.

8. Leary, p. 130; Alfred T. Cox, CS Historical Paper No. 87 History of CAT Vol. 2 April 1969; "Chinese in Burma in Opium-Gun Deal," March 9, 1952, New York Times; "US Gun Runners to Chinese in Burma Profiteering Ex US Fliers," April 8, 1952, *New York Times*.

9. KMT Aggression pp. 183, 188; Information Report, Burma, March 30, 1951, CIA-RDP82-00457R007300480005-8; "Air Base Reported Built by Chiang Unit in Burma," Feb. 22, 1952, *New York Times*.

10. 李先庚 "七載邊荒詩稿──滇緬邊區紀事" "雲南文獻" 第七期；民國66年12月25日出版台北 In English: Li Xiangeng, Seven Years of Borderland Poems *Yunnan Literature*, Dec. 25, 2006, Taipei.

11. Information Report, "Commodity Trends in the Wanting Muse Area," Dec. 30, 1952, CIA-RDP82-00457R015700030008-1; Information Report, "Chinese Communist Dispositions in Yunnan," Feb. 4, 1952, CIA-RDP82-00457R010200430006-9.

12. Uncle Yang Wen Can's consortium, Li Chang Company, was the sole legal agent for petroleum in Kunlong. Eventually, Olive struck out on her own and established the Yang Jin Xiu Yichang Automobile Freight Company. The company existed in various forms until into the 1990s Yang Jinxiu Yichang Automobile Freight Co., Ltd. for large trucks 074-7097810625 臺灣政論 Issues 25–76, 1990, p. 51; the US also sent in technicians and mechanics. The truck trade had become so sensitive that when Lo Hsing Han and Olive were briefly taken into custody while accompanying the first few trucks with a few tons of opium down to Thailand because their vehicle registration looked dubious to the officers. Opium was one of the few things they were trading legally, so they were allowed to continue on to the border after paying a small fine and safely delivered their wares to the traders from Chiang Mai. Illicit Narcotics Traffic: Hearings Before the Subcommittee on Improvements in the Federal Criminal Code of the Committee on the Judiciary, United States Senate, Eighty-fourth Congress, First Session, Pursuant to S. Res. 67 . . . United States: US Government Printing Office, 1955, p. 277. A Dodge with one hundred kilos of opium was seized that year on the way to Mandalay; 臺灣政論 Issues 25–76, 1990, p. 51.

13. 刘清 边纵武装斗争纪实 云南人民出版社 1981, p. 127.

14. Information Report: "Chinese Communist Dispositions in Yunnan," Feb. 4, 1952, CIA-RDP82-00457R010200430006-9; Undated Interim Report on Clandestine Communist Organizations, Part Two, Communist Military Organizations CIA-RDP78-00915R000200130001-4.

15. 刘清 边纵武装斗争纪实 云南人民出版社 1981, p. 126–29

16. Information Report, "Commodity Trends in the Wanting Muse Area," Dec. 30, 1952, CIA-RDP82-00457R015700030008-1.

17. 刘清 边纵武装斗争纪实 云南人民出版社 1981, p. 142.

18. CIA-RDP82-00457R009900200001-4; "Mandalay 'Leaks' Illicit Peiping Aid," Aug. 4, 1951, *New York Times*.

19. 永德县志. China: 云南人民出版社, 1994; Olive appears by name in this document: Information Report: "Commodity Trends in the Wanting Muse Area of the Burma-Yunnan Border," Dec. 30, 1952, CIA-RDP82-00457R015700030008-1.

20. Information Report: "Smuggling Along the Burma China border," Jan. 26, 1952,

21. 李先庚 "七載邊荒詩稿──滇緬邊區紀事" "雲南文獻" 第七期；民國66年12月25日出版台北 In English: Li Xiangeng, Seven Years of Borderland Poems, *Yunnan Literature*, Dec. 25, 2006, Taipei.

22. Information Report: "Political and Military Developments Along the Yunnan Burma Border," March 4, 1952, CIA-RDP82-00457R010500140001-3; Information Report: "Trends in Smuggling along the Burma China Border 1950–1953," July 29, 1953, CIA-RDP80-00810A001800490003-5 . Sai Kham Mong, p. 78.

23. Chieftain of Banhong.

24. 緬甸佤邦勐冒县志. China: 出版者不详, 2002, p. 91; Information Report: "Location of Chinese Nationalist Forces in Burma," May 26, 1953, CIA-RDP80-00810A001300600003-8;

25. 李希哲 Li Xi Zhe.

26. Information Report, "Chinese Communist Dispositions in Yunnan," Feb. 4, 1952, CIA-RDP82-00457R010200430006-9; 人民文學. China: 人民文學出版社, 2001, p. 22–28.

27. Information Report, "Chinese Communist Dispositions in Yunnan," Feb. 4, 1952, CIA-RDP82-00457R010200430006-9; Information Report, "Trends in Smuggling along the Burma China Border 1950–1953," July 1953, CIA-RDP80-00810A001800490003-5; Information Report, "Commodity Trends in the Wanting Muse Area," Dec. 30, 1952, CIA-RDP82-00457R015700030008-1; Information Report, "Trade Routes Between North Burma and China," Aug. 17, 1953, CIA-RDP80-00810A002100220010-2.

28. Information Report: "Strategic Significance of Chinese Communist Road Activity," Feb. 28, 1955, CIA-RDP79T00935A000300150001-5.

29. ."Background on Wa," March 11, 1953, CIA-RDP80-00810A000500440008-0.

30. Information Report, "Background on the Wa," March 11, 1953, CIA-RDP80-00810A000500440008-0.

31. Information Report: "Chinese Nationalist and Communist Activities," July 26, 1953, CIA-RDP80-00810A001700130004-5.

32. "Ruler Chased from Capital," *The Straits Times*, Jan. 29, 1953.

33. Chief of Xiao Hou village in Muse Township. Taungdwin Bo Thein, p. 13; Duan battled a Kachin insurgent named Naw Seng who had retreated to China and received training from communist officials. The battles had played out partially at a hospital complex belonging to American Baptist missionary doctor Gordon Seagrave, Kenton Clymer, "The Trial for High Treason of the 'Burma Surgeon,' Gordon S. Seagrave," *Pacific Historical Review* 81, no. 2 (2012): 245–91.

34. Sai Kham Mong, pp. 122–23. 段榮昌滇籍旅緬三聞僑 《雲南文獻》第26期；民國85年12月25日出版

35. *KMT Aggression*, p. 206.

36. "Burmese Offensives against Chinese Nationalists in Border Area," March 22, 1953, *The Advertiser*, p. 2.

37. Chief Thamin, *Common Life Stories*, Belief Literature, Yangon, 2006, p. 359–61.

38. Sai Kham Mong, pp. 130, 137; Khun Sa, the chieftain's adopted grandson, vowed from that day on to avenge the Secret Army's crimes; *General Khun Sa: His Life and His Speeches*, published by Shan Herald Agency For News DOI, 1989, p. 3.

39. Taungdwin Bo Thein, Page 30; "N'lists Attack Burmese Army Hqrs.," March 13, 1953, *Singapore Standard*.

40. Aung Myoe, "In the Name of Pauk-Phaw: Myanmar's China Policy Since 1948," Singapore, Institute of Southeast Asian Studies, 2011, p. 42; 蔡山, 153.

41. Roughly one thousand men were in three independent detachments in Kokang salaried by the Secret Army; 覃怡輝, p. 441; Information Report Chinese Nationalist Forces in Burma April 15 1953 CIA-RDP80-00810A000900960002-5; "Chiang's Men Seize Prince" *The Singapore Free Press* Aug. 25, 1953, p. 3.

42. To Manglun. Intelligence Report: "Location of Chinese Nationalist Forces in Burma," May 26, 1953, CIA-RDP80-00810A001300600003-8.

43. 蔡山 151–52.

44. German soldiers of the French legion "White with Chinese," April 7, 1953. *Sunday Telegraph News Sydney*, p. 2; "8 Slain by Burmese Rebels," May 18, 1953, *New York Times*.

45. Most of Olive's men stayed behind during the halfhearted evacuation staged with General Chennault's planes, anyway. Gibson, p. 139–51; Clymer, p. 126–31.

46. OCI 4515: "Chinese Communist Forces Reportedly Enter Northeast Burma," July 11, 1953, CIA-RDP91T01172R000200320011-4; "Chinese Reds Assure Rangoon," July 15, 1953, *New York Times*; Information Report, "Chinese Nationalist and Chinese Communist Activities in Shan State," July 1, 1953, CIA-RDP80-00810A001800490004-4; Soviet Press Translations. United States: Far Eastern Institute, University of Washington, 1953, pp. 36–37.

CHAPTER TEN

1. Intelligence Bulletin, Feb. 18, 1954, CIA-15689446; Information Report, "Burmese Pressure on Shan Refugees," June 15, 1954, CIA-RDP80-00810A004300630003-2; "Critical Situations," Dec. 30, 1954, CIA-RDP91T01172R000300170003-9; Burma-China Border Geographic intelligence report July 1954, CIA-RDP79-01009A000700010010-3;

2. Information Report, "Chinese Communist Plan to Establish an Autonomous Shan State," June 17, 1953, CIA-RDP80-00810A001500690003-7.

3. Harold Young, "Paper on the Wa," 1958, unpublished manuscript, family collection of Debbie Young.

4. "Troops Told to Hold off in Burma," Aug. 7, 1956, *New York Times*; "Burmese Assail China," Aug. 29, 1956, *New York Times*; "Red Building Forts," Aug. 26, 1956, *New York Times*; "Burma's Red Frontier," Aug. 3, 1956, *New York Times*; "Burma Invaders Apply Harsh Rule," Aug. 9, 1956, *New York Times*; "Burma Arc Held by Chinese Reds," Aug. 2, 1956, *New York Times*.

5. Harold Young, "Paper on the Wa," 1958, unpublished manuscript, family collection of Debbie Young.

6. 金三角國軍血淚史 (1950–1981), Taiwan: 中央研究院, 2009, p. 363.

7. Patricia Elliott, *The White Umbrella: A Woman's Struggle for Freedom in Burma*, Thailand: Friends Books, 2006, p. 169; Sai Kham Mong, p. 93.

8. The "New Life Movement" or 新生活運動 was a government-led neo-Confucian cultural movement that originated in the Republic of China in the 1930s and was reprised by Chiang Kaishek's government in Taiwan; Yang, p. 129; Sai Kham Mong, p. 92.

9. Zhang Wenhua was Olive's education official at Zhongde Xuexiao. The US embassy also put funding toward their sporting associations through the Asia Foundation. 蔡山, p. 193.

10. Interview with Morton Smith, The Association for Diplomatic Studies and Training Foreign Affairs Oral History Project Information Series, interviewed by Ed Findlay, Nov. 16, 1994.

11. Field Reporter. United States: Division of Publications, Department of State, 1952, p. 27; Dale Carnegie's seminal self-help book *How to Win Friends and Influence People* (1936) eventually became a well-read favorite among Shan dissident groups and was introduced as part of the federal Burmese school curriculum in the 1950s.

12. US National Archives, RG 0306, US Information Agency Information Center Service/Bibliographic Division, 311: Alphabetical Subject Files Containing Policy Guidance Records 1953–1969, Container #4 "Radio Listening and Media Habits in Burma"; USIS provided materials to the psywar department throughout the 1950s, even published an English language magazine circulated among Burma Army officers called *The Open Mind*; US National Archives, RG 0306, US Information Agency Information Center Service/Bibliographic Division, p. 327: Copies of Country Plans, Burma Folder, "Country Plan," March 16, 1959, p. 3.

13. "Young Man's Journey Through Burma," Record Group 111, Mutual Security Agency Films, 1946–1956, 111-MSA-1157, 36065. US National Archives.

14. Department of Defense, "Young Man's Journey Through Burma," [FILM] 1951, NARA ARC Identifier: 36065, US Information Agency also showed an informational film about itself shot in 1954 that included footage of the libraries in Burma. The Gregory Peck film they saw was probably *Purple Plain*. One of Olive's sisters scandalously divorced her husband to marry Kokang Gregory Peck, who became one of Edward's top generals soon thereafter.

15. 缅甸佤邦勐冒县志 p. 28, Feb. 1952, *New York Times*; "Undated Interim Report on Clandestine Communist Organizations, Part Two, Communist Military Organizations," CIA-RDP78-00915R000200130001-4.

16. 缅甸佤邦勐冒县志, pp. 7, 176; "Zhou En Lai Border Report," July 9, 1957, CIA-RDP08C01297R000100190007-6; Information Report: "Local Feeling Toward the Chinese Communists," July 23, 1953, CIA-RDP80-00810A001800490004-4; Burma-China Boundary. United States: Geographer, Office of Research in Economics and Science, Bureau of Intelligence and Research, 1964.

17. 李先庚 "七載邊荒詩稿——滇緬邊區紀事" "雲南文獻" 第七期；民國66年12月25日出版台北 In English: Li Xiangeng, Seven Years of Borderland Poems *Yunnan Literature*, Dec. 25, 2006, Taipei.

18. Ethnic armed work teams 西盟佤族自治县概况. China: 云南民族出版社, 1986, p. 37.

19. 缅甸佤邦勐冒县志. China: 出版者不详, 2002, p. 193.

20. 妇女运动史资料, 1950–2004 沧源瓦族自治县妇女联合会 · 2005; June 17, 1953, Intelligence Report, CIA-RDP80-00810A001500690003-7; Information Report, "Background information on the Wa States," March 11, 1953, CIA-RDP80-00810A000500440008-0.

21. Kuomintang officers Qiu and Chen; 缅甸佤邦勐冒县志. China: 出版者不详, 2002, p. 176–78, 280.

22. "Pressure on Burma Held Peiping's Arm," Aug. 3, 1956, *New York Times*; "Burma Invaders Solidify Position," Aug. 4, 1956, *New York Times.*

23. Yang, p. 74.

24. Hu Kya Shin/Hu Jiagan from Mu Kwan village was told to pay 350 Rupees in fees and was released July 20, 1954. 蔡山 211.

25. Kunlong KutKai Lashio Yang, p. 73; 蔡山, p. 118.

26. Law Si Yan.

27. Sai Kham Mong, p. 79.

28. 匪諜 bandit spy, a historical term used to refer to people who had committed the criminal offense of sedition. The prisoner was Yang De Chen [according to Sai Kham Mong, pp. 91–93], but Judy said it was Peng Jiasheng, who would establish a communist state in Kokang for the Burmese Communist Party, negotiate a ceasefire with Olive in 1989, establish the MDNAA and eventually got purged in 2009.

29. Sai Kham Mong, pp. 91–93. Yang De Chen. But Judy said it was Peng Jiasheng, who would establish a communist state in Kokang for the Burmese Communist Party, negotiate a ceasefire with Olive in 1989, establish the MDNAA, and eventually got purged in 2009.

30. Richard J. Kozicki, "The Sino-Burmese Frontier Problem," Far Eastern Survey, American Institute of Pacific Relations, March 1957; Edward Law Yone, the publisher of *The Nation* and Jimmy's friend was accused of working for the CIA and sued a Soviet newsman. "Burma to Arrest TASS Man," April 29, 1959, New York Times.

31. "Burma Fears Peiping Moves," Aug. 12, 1956, *New York Times*; N. M. Ghatate, "The Sino-Burmese Border Settlement," *India Quarterly 24*, no. 1 (1968): 17–49.

32. The programming had proven such an effective tool at countering the daily communist slogans bleeding from loudspeakers, VOA began providing anti-communist propaganda support to the Burmese Psychological Warfare Directorate department. One of Olive's friends, Aung Gyi, founded the Psychological Warfare Department in 1952; "New Red Incursion in Burma Reported," Sept. 17, 1956, *New York Times.*

33. Review of Hong Kong Chinese Press. Hong Kong: n.p., 1958, p. 23; "Communist China Broadcasting Bureau," Dec. 1960, CIA-RDP78-02646R000100090001-7.

34. Sai Kham Mong, p. 91–93.

35. Near Wanting.

36. Illicit Narcotics Traffic: Hearings Before the Subcommittee on Improvements in the Federal Criminal Code of the Committee on the Judiciary, United States Senate, Eighty-fourth Congress, First Session, Pursuant to S. Res. 67 . . . United States: US Government Printing Office, 1955, p. 106.

37. Gibson, p. 31; "Burmese Fight Rebels," May 12, 1955, *New York Times*; The sawmill was near Taunggyi The Yunnan Provincial Trading Company helped them trade; Information Report "Chinese Nationalist Road Repair and Construction," June 16, 1954, CIA-RDP80-00810A004300360003-2.

38. The story of the murder at the logging enterprise was likely conflated with other stories. A high-ranking Secret Army officer named Li Guo Hui (credited with recruiting

Olive) stood trial for murdering a deputy and floating his body down the river. Fat Huang (Huang Dalong) was said to have killed his deputy Huang Tianyou, but it's unclear if Olive ordered the killing directly or Fat Huang took it upon himself to do it. 覃怡輝 p. 455.

39. Gerald Sparrow, *Land of the Moonflower*, United Kingdom, Elek Books, 1955, p. 76–78. The employment roster at the Court Museum of Thailand in Bangkok lists John Walter Gerald Sparrow as a legal advisor to the International Court from B.E.2472-2482 (1929–1939).

40. The Department of State Bulletin. United States: Office of Public Communication, Bureau of Public Affairs, 1954, p. 369; Gerald Sparrow, *Women Who Murder*, Tower Books, London, 1970; Gerald Sparrow, *Queens of Crime*, Tower Books, London, 1973; "So Black Tiger Died," *Argus* Melbourne, April 15, 1956.

41. Gerald Sparrow, *Lawyer at Large*, J. Long, London, 1960, p. 117.

42. "On the Trail of Dope Runners," Nov. 12, 1955, *Perth Mirror*; Gerald Sparrow, *Lawyer at Large*, John Long Limited, London, 1960, p. 120. It eventually emerged Sparrow financially supported apartheid propaganda through the Club of Ten; "Thai opium informants Paid," Sept. 22, 1955, *New York Times*.

43. Intelligence Report Travel to Cheli May 5, 1955, CIA-RDP80-00810A006700650008-2; "China Nationalists Stir Up East Burma," Feb 21, 1955, *New York Times*; "Nationalists Reported in Laos," March 9, 1955, *New York Times*; "Chinese Retake Burmese Town," March 21, 1955, *New York Times*; Sai Kham Mong, p. 93.

44. Gerald Sparrow, *Opium Venture*, United Kingdom, R. Hale, 1957, p. 16.

45. *Opium Venture, Loc 575. Winnington, 58, 127, 137; Harold Young, Harold. "Paper on the Wa," 1958, Unpublished manuscript, Family collection, Debbie Young.*

46. Sai Kham Mong, p. 91–92. Jimmy's businesses included the East Burma Bank Ltd. and the Shwe Baho Cinema, as well as the country's first steam laundry. When Olive had a business license revoked as punishment for operating an illegal chain of gambling dens in Kokang, Jimmy helped Olive operate on his export licenses as a workaround, so the planes could keep coming Edward and Jimmy were finally forced to revoke Olive's business licenses, on penalty of losing their own.

47. Olive bought Wah Wah a canary-yellow Chevrolet, because Wah Wah's name meant yellow in Burmese. For further reading about Louisa Benson: Charmaine Craig, *Miss Buma*, Grove Atlantic, 2017.

48. Uncle Charlie's wife and other; 蔡山, p. 26.

49. Gerald Sparrow, *Not Wisely But Too Well*, United Kingdom, G. G. Harrap, 1961, p. 72.

50. *Land of the Moonflower*, p. 225.

51. "Probe into Report on Dope Ring in Singapore," July 12, 1959, *Straits Times*, p. 5; Reports and Documents. United States: n.p., 1958, p. 760; Police chief Phao Siyanon was ousted in an unrelated coup that coincidentally happened around when *Opium Venture* was published.

CHAPTER TWELVE

1. Sterling Seagrave, *Lords of the Rim*, United Kingdom, Putnam's Sons, 1995, p. 346.

2. 云南省阿昌族社会历史调查材料 阿昌族調查資料 · Volume 1 中国科学院民族研究所云南民族調查組. 1963, p. 24.

3. 萧德虎，镇康县志，四川民族出版社 1992, p. 699.

4. 蔡山, 157, 254; CIA Office of National Estimates, "Forged Documents Communist Rebellion," March 1957, CIA-RDP79T00937A000500030045-6李學華，走過金三角. Taiwan: 秀威資訊科技股份有限公司, 2008, p. 63.

5. Sai Kham Mong, p. 96.

6. 中國大陸研究, Issue 84, July 1972 。中國大陸問題研究所, p. 10; "Border Dispute Worries Burma," June 26, 1957, *New York Times*. Following a border conference of the Shan and Kachin peoples, held in Yunnan and attended by both the Chinese and Burmese Premiers, some Shan leaders prepared for secession.

7. Sai Kham Mong, p. 95; "Burmese Disappointed," Dec. 21, 1956, *New York Times*, p. 8.

8. There were 280 Kokang recruits. Sai Kham Mong, p. 180.

9. Sai Kham Mong, p. 94. There were 280 Kokang recruits. "Tibet Stirs Burmese," April 5, 1959, *New York Times*.

10. "Red China Protests to Burma on Raids," Nov. 27, 1958, *New York Times*.

11. 覃怡輝, p. 284.

12. James T. Fisher, *Dr. America: The Lives of Thomas A. Dooley, 1927–1961*, Boston, University of Massachusetts Press, 1998, p. 82.

13. McCoy, pp. 308–10, 341. U Ba Thein was Harold's recruit who founded the 16 Musketeers. The monk was named Gnar Kham. Sao Khun Seik also arrived.

14. "The Pattern of Communist Propaganda Concerning Laos 1955–1956," March 1957, CIA-RDP78-00915R000600080007-0; Thomas Dooley, *The Night They Burned the Mountain Down*, Farrar Strauss and Giroux, New York, 1960, p. 92. "Is US Aid Buying Cars for Laotians," March 11, 1958, *New York Mirror*.

15. Sai Kham Mong, p. 99. Commander of the 6th Brigade stationed in Lashio; Robert Taylor, *General Ne Win a Political Biography*, ISEAS Publishing Singapore, 2015, p. 35.

16. 280 Kokang recruits Sai Kham Mong, p. 94.

17. Sai Kham Mong, pp. 96–97. Brigadier San Yu and Ne Win on May 17.

18. "Burmese Seize Plants," May 20, 1959, *New York Times*.

19. 280 Kokang recruits Sai Kham Mong, p. 94.

20. "New Revolt in Burma," April 28, 1959, *Singapore Standard*, p. 1. No More Rights," Feb. 5, 1959, *The Singapore Free Press*; U.P.I $15 million compensation Feb. 12.15 times their annual tax incomes; "Revolt in Shan State," Nov. 28, 1959, *The Singapore Free Press*, p. 3; *November 1959*; "Burmese Drive on Rebels," Nov. 29, 1959, *New York Times*; "Uprising in Shan State Crushed," Dec. 5, 1959, *The Singapore Free Press*. Reuter Microfilm Reel NL2458p. 1; Central Intelligence Bulletin, June 19, 1959. CIA-5B15787495-5D.

21. "Reds Cross into Burma," Jun. 1, 1959, *New York Times*; "Red Incursion Alleged," Nov. 2, 1959, *New York Times*; "Burma, Red China at Odds on Border," Sept. 8, 1959, *New York Times*.

22. Taungdwin Bo Thein, p. 27; Central Intelligence Bulletin 15787529 April 14, 1959, CIA-5B15787529.

23. "Ant Battle Witnessed," Oct. 17, 1959, *New York Times*.

24. *Burma Weekly Bulletin*, Myanmar (Burma): n.p., May 28, 1959, p. 46. "Burma Quells Revolt," Dec. 5, 1959, *New York Times*; "Parliament dissolved," Dec. 21, 1959, *New York Times*.

25. Jan. 17, 1960. Sai Kham Mong, p. 99; Yang, p. 77.

26. "Lai pang vai!"

27. Harold Young, Harold. "Paper on the Wa," 1958, Uunpublished manuscript, Family collection, Debbie Young.

28. 缅甸佤邦勐冒县志. pp. 7, 182, 232.

29. Wa villagers robbed of their silver were convinced the caravan traders had plotted to share the spoils and retaliated by beheading one of them. They tried to negotiate the return of the loot, but it was too late. The feud was so fierce that anybody could be beheaded at any time, Wa or not. 缅甸佤邦勐冒县志. China: 出版者不详, 2002, p. 194.

30. 走過金三角.Taiwan: 秀威資訊科技股份有限公司, 2008, p. 227; Intelligence Bulletin, Dec. 28, 1960, CIA-5B15798730; "Boundary Treaty Between the People's Republic of China and the Union of Burma," Oct. 1, 1960, CIA-RDP08C01297R000100190005-8.

31. 缅甸佤邦勐冒县志 91. Na Cheng district.

32. 蔡山, 180。

33. "Chinese Repulsed in Burma," Jan. 12, 1961, *New York Times*.

34. "Complaint by Burma of Aggression by the Government of the Republic of China," January 1, 1961.

35. "10,000 in Rangoon Riot against US," Feb. 22, 1961, *New York Times*; U Nu letter of April 29, 1961. JFKPOF-112a-007-p0016 John F. Kennedy Presidential Library and Museum.

36. Treasury-Post Office Departments and Executive Office Appropriations for 1964 Treasury Department [and] Related Agencies: Hearings Before a Subcommittee of the Committee on Appropriations, House of Representatives, Eighty-eighth Congress, First Session, p. 471.

37. Gordon Young, *Run for the Mountains*, XLibris, p. 138; Gordon Young, *Journey From Banna*, XLibris, 2011, US, p. 25; Mccoy, pp. 339–41.

38. Interview with Bill Lair, OH0200. Vietnam Center and Sam Johnson Vietnam Archive,. 11 Dec. 11, 2001, Bill Lair Collection, Vietnam Center and Sam Johnson Vietnam Archive, Texas Tech University, https://www.vietnam.ttu.edu/virtualarchive/items.php?item=OH0200; "Nationalists Fighting in Laos Civil War," May 23, 1961, *New York Times*; "CIA Backed Laotians Said Entering China for Radio Surveillance," Jan. 26, 1971, *Washington Post*.

39. 李學華, 走過金三角. Taiwan: 秀威資訊科技股份有限公司, 2008, pp. 158–60; Office of Current Intelligence, "Chinese Nationalist Irregulars in the Thai-Laotian-Burmese Border Area," May 17, 1963, CIA-RDP79T00429A001100040024-5.

40. Ne Win had staged a coup in 1958 as a result of a suspected assassination plot. He handed power back over to the civilian government after an election in 1960. "Burma Lists Ministers," Oct. 15, 1958, *New York Times*.

41. Yang, p. 89.

42. On Feb. 8, 1963, U Aung Gyi was dismissed. "Ford Group Moves Halt Foundation," Jun. 17, 1962, *New York Times*; "All Burmese Colleges Shut," July 10, 1962, *New York Times*; "Burma Cracks Down on Travelers," July 16, 1959, *Singapore Free Press*.

43. Seymour Topping, "Rangoon Losing Prominence," Dec. 20, 1963, *New York Times*;

44. When a Kokang soldier was murdered in retaliation within the week, Olive arranged for a big funeral. Though it had not been intended as a protest, thousands came to mourn publicly in the market, marching proudly past the intimidated Burmese sentries.蔡山, p. 153.

45. John A. Williams, Harry Jacob Anslinger, J. Dennis Gregory, *The Protectors: The Heroic Story of the Narcotics Agents, Citizens, and Officials in Their Unending, Unsuing Battles Against Organized Crime in America and Abroad*, United States: Farrar, Straus, and Girous, 1964, pp. 242–44; *Organized Crime and Illicit Traffic in Narcotics*, Washington, DC, US Government Printing Office, 1963, pp. 710–12.

CHAPTER THIRTEEN

1. Felix Belair Jr., "CIA identifies 21 Asian opium refineries," Jun. 6, 1971, *New York Times*, p. 2; "Sharp Rise in Addicts Spurs Burmese to Act Against Huge Narcotics Trade," Sept. 13, 1973, *New York Times*.

2. Embassy Bangkok to Secretary of State, Telegram R 151015Z, January 15, 1974, R151015Z9752JAN74 Central Foreign Policy Files, 1973–79/Electronic Telegrams, RG 59: General Records of the Department of State, US National Archives; Organized Crime and Illicit Traffic in Narcotics. United States: US Government Printing Office, 1963.

3. "CIA Secretly Runs 30,000 Group in Laos," Sept. 15, 1971, Canberra Times, 1970.

4. Embassy Bangkok to Secretary of State, Telegram, R 081220Z February 1974, R 081220Z458FEB74 Central Foreign Policy Files, 1973– 79/Electronic Telegrams, RG 59: General Records of the Department of State, US National Archives.

5. To Embassy Bangkok, Embassy Rangoon, Telegram, 1974STATE034770, February 21, 1974.

6. "Opium King is Returned," Aug. 6, 1973, Canberra Times.

7. Embassy Bangkok to Secretary of State, Telegram, R 190726Z FEB 74 R 190726ZFEB 747701 Central Foreign Policy Files, 1973– 79/Electronic Telegrams, RG 59: General Records of the Department of State, US National Archives.

8. Olive and Francis's cousin Donald, who was later assassinated in the middle of a restaurant before his food had even arrived by Lo Hsing Han's brother in Chiang Mai, in December 1979.

9. Khin Nyunt.

10. In 1989, Peng Jiasheng mutineed and the Communist Party of Burma split. Lo Hsing Han had been counseling the government on their ceasefires but was not a trusted figure in Kokang. Khin Nyunt saw in Olive a power broker who would win the confidence of Kokang people who had good reason to be suspicious of outsiders.

11. Ever since they became Senior General Than Shwe's favored militia. The recently retired dictator earned his stripes by fighting campaigns against Kokang rebels in the seventies when he moved to Kutkai In 1972, Than Shwe, and became the regional commander for the 88th Light Infantry Division in Shan State in Monse/Narle in Northern Shan State, Kengtung/Mong and Khat/Mongoung east of the Salween. Senior General

Than Shwe donated a pagoda in Duan's village, claimed he viewed them as blood brothers, and vowed to include their ethnically Chinese group as citizens of Myanmar and was
shot in battle. As he was near death from his injuries, one of Duan's militia leaders who
happened to have the same blood type stepped in to save his life. Ever since then, their
militia has enjoyed special business concessions. *Tamuying Mong Wong Ethnic Group and
its History* Taungdwin Bo Thein, Lashio, 2003, p. 23. Accessed at the Lashio Museum for
Ethnic Minorities.

12. 卸甲妆凤仪弯配勐稳土司·真乃京兆贤淑良母德教传家风横刀跨骏骑驰骋
怒江东西·不愧果敢巾帼枭雄英名齐北掉

Bibliography

ABN Correspondence. Germany: Press Bureau of the AntiBolshevik Bloc of Nations, 1970.

Asian Folklore Studies. Japan: Nanzan University Institute of Anthropology, 1963.

Beamish, John. *Burma Drop.* Elek Books. New York. 1958.

Belanger, Francis W. *Drugs, the U.S., and Khun Sa.* Thailand: Editions Duang Kamol, 1989.

Bo Thein, Taungdwin. *Tamuying Mong Wong Ethnic Group and its History.* Lashio, 2003. Accessed at the Lashio Museum for Ethnic Minorities.

Braund, Harold Ernest W. *Tales of Burma.* United Kingdom: J. Paton, 1981.

Chennault, Claire Lee. *Way of a Fighter: Memoirs of General Claire Lee Chennault.* G. P. Putnam's Sons, New York, 1949.

Clymer, Kenton. *A Delicate Relationship: The United States and Burma/Myanmar Since 1945.* Ithaca, NY: Cornell University Press, 2015.

Clymer, Kenton. "The Trial for High Treason of the 'Burma Surgeon,' Gordon S. Seagrave." *Pacific Historical Review* 81, no. 2 (2012): 245–91.

Craig, Charmaine. *Miss Burma.* Grove Atlantic, 2017.

Conant, Jennet. *A Covert Affair: The Adventures of Julia and Paul Child in the OSS.* Simon and Schuster New York, 2011.

Cox, Alfred T. CS Historical Paper No. 87 History of CAT Vol. 2, April 1969.

Curtiss, Jack Samson. *Flying Tiger: The True Story of General Claire Chennaul and the US 14th Air Force in China.* Lyons Press, 2011.

Donnison, F. S. V British Military Administration in the Far East, 1943–46. United Kingdom: H.M. Stationery Office, 1956.

Dooley, Thomas. *The Night They Burned the Mountain Down.* New York: Farrar Strauss and Giroux, 1960.

Drage, Godfrey. *A Few Notes on Wa.* Superintendent Government Printing Press of Burma, 1907.

Duckett, Richard. *Spiers Mission: The Special Operations Executive in Burma.* London: IB Tauris Co. Ltd., 2018.

Elliott, Patricia. *The White Umbrella: A Woman's Struggle for Freedom in Burma.* Thailand: Friends Books, 2006.

Fisher, James T. *Dr. America: The Lives of Thomas A. Dooley, 1927–1961.* United States: University of Massachusetts Press, 1998.

Fairbanks, John King. *The Cambridge History of China: Volume 8, The Ming Dynasty 1368–1644.* Cambridge University Press, 1978.

General Khun Sa: His Life and His Speeches, published by Shan Herald Agency For News DOI, 1989.

Gibson, Richard Michael and Chen, Wen H. *The Secret Army: Chiang Kai-shek and the Drug Warlords of the Golden Triangle.* Wiley, 2011.

Hee, Puck L. "Travels in Kokang," *The Guardian,* Vol. 12 No. 5.1958. Rangoon.

Is Trust Vindicated? A Chronicle of the Various Accomplishments of the Government Headed by General Ne Win During the Period of Tenure from November, 1958 to February 6, 1960. Myanmar (Burma): n.p., 1960.

Jaiyen, Khuensai. "Kokang Question," *Thai-Yunnan Project Newsletter,* Issue 12, 1991, p. 3.

Kam Mong, Sai. *Kokang and Kachin in the Shan States (1945–1960).* Chulalongkorn University Press, 2011.

Khaing, Mi Mi. *Kanbawsa: A Modern Review.* Rangoon: The Nation Publishing, 1949.

Kozicki, Richard J. *International Relations of South Asia 1947–80.* N.p.: n.p., 1981.

Kratoska, Paul H. *Southeast Asian Minorities in the Wartime Japanese Empire.* New York: Routledge Curzon, 2002.

Kratoska, Paul H. *Southeast Asian Minorities in the Wartime Japanese Empire.* New York: Routledge Curzon, 2002.

Kuhn, Isobel. *Green Leaf in Drought: The Story of the Escape of the Last C.I.M. Missionaries from Communist China.* Singapore: Overseas Missionary Fellowship, 1983.

Lamour, Catherine. *Enquête sur une Armée Secrète.* Seuil, Paris, 1975, 21.

Leary, William. *Perilous Missions: Civil Air Transport and CIA Operations in Asia.* University of Alabama Press, 1984.

Lee, Puck Hee. *In the Land of Awesome Kings.* N.p.: Cork Hill Press, 2004.

Lin Myat, Zaw. "Heritage in the Myanmar Frontier: Shan State Haws and the Conditions for Public Participation," Columbia University, May 2017, New York. Submitted in partial fulfillment of MS for Historic Preservation.

Lintner, Bertil. *The Golden Triangle Opium Trade: An Overview Chiang Mai.* Asia Pacific Media Services, March 2000.

Marshall, Jonathan. "Opium and the Politics of Gangsterism in Nationalist China," *Critical Asian Studies Journal* Vol. 8 No. 3, 1976.

Marshall, Jonathan. "Opium and the Politics of Gangsterism in Nationalist China," *Bulletin of Concerned Asian Scholars,* Vol. 8, No. 3.

Massari, Reverend B. "Silver Jubilee of Saint Joseph's Convent," *Catholic Missions* Vol. 15–16, Aug. 1922, Society for the Propagation of the Faith, New York, p. 181.

Maung Maung, U. *Burma in the Family of Nations.* Netherlands: Institute of Pacific Relations, 1957.

McCoy, Alfred. *The Politics of Heroin.* Lawrence Hill Books, 1972.

Ministry of Information. *Kuomintang Aggression Against Burma,* Burma Information and Broadcasting Department, Rangoon, 1953.

Mitton, Geraldine Edith. *In the Grip of the Head Hunters.* Black Inc. London. 1923.

Mongrai, Saimong. *The Shan States and the British Annexation.* Cornell University Press, 1965.

Myint-U, Thant. *River of Lost Footsteps*. New York: Farrar, Straus and Giroux, 2006.

Naing, Htun. *The Kokang People of the Upper Reaches of the Salween River*. Self-published in Yangon, 2012, p. 45.

Organized Crime and Illicit Traffic in Narcotics. United States: US Government Printing Office, 1963.

Robbins, Christpher. *Air America: The History of the CIA's Secret Airline*. New York: G.P. Putnam's Sons, 1979.

Ronco, Daniele. "Il maggio di santa Oliva origin della forma sviluppo della tradizione," ETS, Pisa University, 2001.

Sai Aung Htun. *A History of the Shan State from its Origin to 1963*. Bangkok: Silkworm Books, 2009.

Sanda, Sao. *The Moon Princess: Memories of the Shan States*. Bangkok: River Books, 2008.

Scott, Sir James Goerge. *Burma: A Handbook of Practical Information*. London: The De La More Press. 1906.

Scott, James George and Hardiman, John Percy. *Gazetteer of Upper Burma and the Shan States*, 1899.

Seagrave, Gordon. *Burma Surgeon*. Norton and Company, 1943.

Seagrave, Sterling. *The Marcos Dynasty*. New York: Harper and Row, 1988.

Seagrave, Sterling. *Lords of the Rim*. United Kingdom: Putnam's Sons, 1995.

Seymour Topping. *Journey Between Two Chinas*. New York: Harper and Row, 1972, p. 129.

Slack, Edward R. *Opium, State, and Society: China's Narco-Economy and the Guomindang, 1924–1937*. Honolulu: University of Hawai'i Press, 2001.

Sola, Richard. *Chine-Birmanie, histoire d'une guerre secrète: 1949–1954*. France: Sudestasie, 1990.

Soviet Press Translations. United States: Far Eastern Institute, University of Washington, 1953.

Sparrow, Gerald. *Land of the Moonflower*. United Kingdom: Elek Books, 1955.

Sparrow, Gerald. *Opium Venture*. United Kingdom: R. Hale, 1957.

Sparrow, Gerald. *Lawyer at Large*. London: John Long Limited, 1960.

Taylor, Robert. *General Ne Win: A Political Biography*. ISEAS Publishing Singapore, 2015, p. 35.

Taylor, Robert. *Foreign and Domestic Consequences of the KMT in Burma*. Ithaca, NY: Cornell University Press, 1973.

Tegenfeldt, Herman G. *A Century of Growth: the Kachin Baptist Church of Burma*. United States: William Carey Library, 1974.

Thamin. *Common Life Stories*. Belief Literature, Yangon, 2006, pp. 359–61.

Wiener, Tim. *Betrayal: The Story of Aldrich Ames, an American Spy*. New York: Penguin Random House, 1995.

Yang, Bo. "Golden Triangle: Frontier and Wilderness." Translation by Clive Gulliver. Hong Kong: Joint Publishing Co., 1997.

Yang, Bo, *Alien Realm*. Taipei, 1961. Translated by Janice J Yu. Janus Publishing Company, London, 1996.

Yang, Li. *House of Yang*. Sydney: Bookpress, 1997.

Young. Gordon. *Run for the Mountains*. XLibris, USA.

Young, Gordon. *Journey From Banna*. XLibris, 2011, USA.

Young, Harold. "Paper on the Wa," 1958, Unpublished manuscript, family collection of Debbie Young.

蔡山 果敢志 天马出版社 香港 2012.

李學華， 走過金三角. Taiwan: 秀威資訊科技股份有限公司, 2008.

李先庚 "七載邊荒詩稿——滇緬邊區紀事" "雲南文獻" 第七期；民國66年12月25日 出版台北

云南省阿昌族社会历史调查材料 阿昌族调查資料·Volume 1 中国科学院民族研究所云南民族调查組. 1963.

萧德虎，镇康县志，四川民族出版社 1992.

永德县志. China: 云南人民出版社, 1994.

缅甸佤邦勐冒县志. China: 出版者不详, 2002.

西盟佤族自治县概况. China: 云南民族出版社, 1986.

李明富. 沧源佤族自治县志，云南民族出版社, 1998.

佤族历史文化研究. China: 社会科学文献出版社·人文分社, 2018.

妇女运动史资料, 1950–2004 沧源瓦族自治县妇女联合会·2005

刘清 边纵武装斗争纪实 云南人民出版社 1981.

金三角: 我与地方武装的生死之交. China: 上海远东出版社, 2011.

金三角國軍血淚史(1950–1981). Taiwan: 中央研究院, 2009.

覃怡輝 金三角國軍血淚史：*1950–1981*·中央研究院 2009.

程景 金三角风云(泰国坤沙贩毒集团) 北方文艺出版社, Beijing, 2018.

博尊宝 信仰如血 天马出版有限公司。2013.

臺灣文獻叢刊. Taiwan: 臺灣銀行, 1957.

方天建：缅甸勐稳华人身份本土化问题研究 《世界民族》(京)2018年第1期；

杨煜达 清代中期滇边银矿的矿民集团与边疆秩序 中国边疆史地研究. 2016.

革非. 中国远征军女兵缅甸蒙难记. China: 北京市燕山出版社, 1992.

Index

family contrasted with, 33, 41,
65, 120
Lone Army. *See* Yunnan Anti-
communist National Salvation
Army
Lords of the Sky (*sawbwas*),
49, 185n10; in Chamber
of Nationalities, 187n15;
retirement bonus rejected by,
157; retirement forced upon,
158–59; titles relinquished by,
156
Lu Chengwang, xi
Lu Shwin Zhen, *41*, 183n36
Lynn (grand-niece), 39–43

Ma Khin Nyunt, 53
man, Yang, O., compared with, 75,
119, 135
Mandalay prison, Yang, O., in, 114,
118
Mao Zedong, 49
march, Yang, O., leading, 135–36
marriage, with Yang, O., 69,
185n5; to cousin, 68; to
Duan C., 54–55, 57, 184n2;
heir required by, 51–52; to
Wah Wah, 166–67; Yang, O.
avoiding, 46
Mekong River, *103*, *155*
messenger, Yang, O., jailing, 136
Miao people, 183n16
Min Aung Hlaing, 5, 181n5
mines, in Wa states, 23, 56, 128,
129, 134

Ming dynasty, 20, 21
Miss Hairy Legs (*Nang Kha Khon*)
(pseudonym), 11–14, 35,
42–43, 145
MNDAA. *See* Myanmar National
Democratic Alliance Army
Mong Hsat, Burma, 80–81, 107
Mongmao, Wa states, 83
Mongshu, Secret Army infiltrating,
113
morphine, 183n18
mother, of Yang, O., 15, 19, 25–26,
51, 60
Mother Superior, expelling Yang,
O., 28
mules, Huang taking, 104–5
Muong Sing, Laos, *155*, 158
murder, by Yang, O., 64
Muse, Myanmar, *3*, 36–37, *50*,
147–48
Muslims, Rohingya, 10
Myanmar, *82*, 92; Academy
Awards of, 122; censorship in,
4, 6–8; China contrasted with,
37; civil wars in, 11; Muse
in, *3*, 36–37, *50*, 147–48;
National Archives of, x–xi;
Yang family in, 14; Yangon
in, xv, 1, 6, 39, 62, *66*. *See also*
borders, of Myanmar; Burma;
citizenship, in Myanmar;
Kokang, Myanmar; Shan
state, Myanmar
Myanmar military, 11; censorship
favoring, 6, 7; Kokang

107; against Burma Army, 115, 140; CIA supporting, 35, 158; incursion by, *82*; in Kokang, 85, 192n41; Mongshu infiltrated by, 113; Ne Win allowing, 75; People's Liberation Army attacking, 164; roads targeted by, 109; on Savage Mountain, 83; US withdrawing, 164; Yang, O., romanticized by, 73–74; Yunnan targeted by, 76, 81, 84

Zhang Fu Chu, 186n13
Zhang Wenhua, 192n9